60

Andrew Cruickshank's

Scottish
Bedside Book

JOHNSTON and BACON
London and Edinburgh

A Johnston & Bacon book published by
Cassell & Collier Macmillan Publishers Ltd.
35 Red Lion Square, London WC1R 4SG
& Tanfield House, Tanfield Lane, Edinburgh EH3 5LL
and at Sydney, Auckland, Toronto, Johannesburg,
an affiliate of
Macmillan Publishing Co.
New York

© Johnston & Bacon,
a division of Cassell & Collier Macmillan
Publishers Ltd., 1977

First Published 1977

ISBN 0 7179 4224 4

Printed in Great Britain by
The Camelot Press Ltd, Southampton

Contents

The Mosaic

Acknowledgements

For permission to reprint material the following acknowledgements are made.
FOR EXTRACTS: from *She Had a Magic* by B. O'Brien, to Ad Schulberg
Agency, the author and Jonathan Cape Ltd; from *New Letters and Memorials
of Jane Welsh Carlyle* edited by Alexander Carlyle published by The Bodley
Head, to the publisher; from *James Clerk Maxwell: a commemoration volume*,
to Cambridge University Press; from *The Men who Ruled India* by P.
Woodruff to the author and Jonathan Cape Ltd; from *The Life of Burns* by C.
Carswell, to John Carswell and Chatto & Windus; from *Autobiography of
Andrew Carnegie* and *Moral Plays* by J. Bridie, to Constable & Co. Ltd; from
The Law of Scotland by H. Levy-Ullmann, to W. Green & Son Ltd; from
Fleming: Discoverer of Penicillin by L. J. Ludovici, to The Hamlyn Publishing
Group Ltd; from *On Translation* edited by R. A. Brower, to Harvard University
Press; from *The Declaration of Arbroath, The Last Letter of Mary Queen of
Scots* and *Scotland Today*, to the Controller of Her Majesty's Stationery Office;
from *Kelvin the Man* by A. G. King, to Hodder & Stoughton Ltd; from *Sunset
Song* by L. G. Gibbon, to Hutchinson Publishing Group Ltd; from *An Indian
Summer* by J. Cameron, *Biography of Viscount Bryce* by H. A. L. Fisher and
Highways and Byways in the West Highlands by S. Gordon, to Macmillan
London and Basingstoke; from *Glasgow University's Pictures* by A. M. Young,
to Professor Miles; from *Golfer's Handbook*, to Munro-Barr Publications Ltd;
from *James Maxton: The Portrait of a Rebel* by G. McAlister, to John Murray
(Publishers) Ltd, from *Types of Modern Theology* by H. R. Mackintosh, to
James Nisbet & Co. Ltd; from *Gargantua* by Rabelais, translated by Sir
Thomas Urquhart and P. Le Motteux, published by Oxford University Press
(1934). Reprinted by permission of the publisher; from *History of Scotland* by
J. D. Mackie, pp. 259–61. © J. D. Mackie, 1964. Reprinted by permission of
Penguin Books Ltd; from *Remembrance of Things Past* by Marcel Proust,
translated by C. K. Scott Moncrieff. Copyright 1929 and renewed 1957 by
Random House, Inc. Reprinted by permission of the publisher, the translator's
Literary Estate and Chatto & Windus; from *Montrose* by John Buchan, to
Susan, Lady Tweedsmuir; from *The Rise and Fall of British Documentary* by E.
Sussex. Copyright © 1975 by the Regents of the University of California;
reprinted by permission of the University of California Press; from *Boswell in
Extremes, 1776–1778* edited by C. M. Weiss and F. A. Pottle. Copyright ©
1970 by Yale University. Reprinted by permission of Yale University, William

Heinemann Ltd and McGraw-Hill Book Co. FOR POEMS: *Wedding*, to George Mackay Brown; *Aberdeen Child*, to George Bruce; *Hamewith* from *Collected Poems* by Sidney Goodsir Smith, to John Calder (Publishers) Ltd; *Hamewith* from *Hamewith and Other Poems* by Charles Murray, to Constable & Co. Ltd; *Warriors*, to Douglas Dunn; *The Scot's Lament* by Kitty Kennedy Allen and Kennedy Allen from *The Old Time Stars' Book of Monologues*. © 1929. Published by Reynolds Music. Reproduced by permission of EMI Music Publishing Ltd, 138–140 Charing Cross Road, London WC2H 0LD; *Bedtime*, to Ian Hamilton Finlay; *Lassie, What Mair Wad You Hae* by Sir Alexander Gray, to John Gray; *Speaking of Scotland* from *The Run from Life* by Maurice Lindsay, to the author and Cygnet Press; *Old Edinburgh* from *A Man in My Position* by Norman MacCaig, reprinted by permission of the author and The Hogarth Press Ltd; *Anent the Deeference o Tastes* from *Wi the Haill Voice* by Edwin Morgan. © Edwin Morgan, 1972, to the author and Carcanet New Press Ltd; *The Heart Could Never Speak* from *Collected Poems* by Edwin Muir. Copyright © 1960 by Willa Muir. Reprinted by permission of Oxford University Press, Inc. and Faber & Faber Ltd; *For the Old Highlands* by Douglas Young, to F. F. Sharles & Co.; *To Have Found One's Country, John Knox* and *Culloden and After*, to Ian Crichton Smith. FOR ILLUSTRATIONS: *Sea Quest*, photograph by British Petroleum; *Jane Welsh Carlyle*, from Carlyle's house, a property of the National Trust; *Mary Slessor*, to Church of Scotland Overseas Council; *The Scott Monument and Edinburgh Castle*, to Edinburgh City Libraries; *Chair, Daily Record Buildings, Girls at Play* and *Dr William Hunter*, to Hunterian Art Gallery, University of Glasgow; *MacDonell of Glengarry*, to National Gallery of Scotland; *Tom Morris's Gravestone*, to North East Fife District Council; *Sir Alexander Fleming*, to St Mary's Hospital Medical School; *Montrose* and *Finlay of Colonsay*, to Scottish National Portrait Gallery.

Every effort has been made to contact copyright holders. Where this has not been possible, the publishers wish to tender apologies and thanks.

Preface

An invitation to compile a Bedside Book has the effect—as Dr Johnson's felon under judgement appreciated in other circumstances—of wonderfully concentrating the mind. And a Scottish Bedside Book at that. As I peer round my native land, an increasing familiarity with its resource and diversity engenders humility. Where to begin? Who's in, who's out? How to compound the mystery of things that has brought these people together in this particular space of the globe, and convey something of their distinctiveness?

I may find comfort as a maker of books from St Bonaventura who suggested that 'a man may write the works of others with additions, and he is called a "compiler" (compilator)'. To Bonaventura in the thirteenth century the world was Europe, the language in the main Latin, and on Easter Sunday from Cork to Cracow it is possible that a devout Christian would feel himself spiritually at home anywhere.

But in the twentieth century, what is a Bedside Book? Its position ensures that it will never be a central consideration: no politician will sell his policy by it, no theologian will guide your destiny by it, and for the lover it is a playful deceit. And yet it is precisely for these shortcomings that a Scotsman may lend his time and attention to suggest something by way of a whisper, a footnote or a parenthesis, that the inhabitants of Scotland are not to be categorised as simply beasts for sale in the market.

There is for instance the illusion held by the best people in the highest places (I mean of course the ancient English universities) that we are either irredeemably barbaric or incurably romantic. Whatever the truth, the people in these islands have one thing in common—they are Europeans. A compiler then, in self-defence, might justifiably turn to Greece for a model for his project.

It was Homer who first set the pattern of European art by

9

recognising the duality that lay at the heart of all life and experience; and expressed in concrete literature the insight that life moves in a line or lies about us as in a mosaic. Ulysses wandered twenty years round the Mediterranean in an extended 'line' to find, almost unrecognisable, his Penelope; and the Iliad is composed of a 'mosaic' as Greek and Trojan wrestle with the circumstance of the last year of a ten years' war sparked off by a childish quarrel.

We are at a unique moment in time. In our infinite smallness the gifts of a gene and an environment are all we inherit from the past, and we live in a present which contains an entirely new diversity due to man's ranging imagination. If he would retain his balance in this diverse world, a man might well turn to Homer for his initial model of understanding. If this is my model, what goals might I aim at?

My project was clear enough; to become as good an actor as I could given such gifts as I was born with, and more important as I grew in experience, my limitations. As an actor I was presented with an amazing richness, the whole European literature of tragedy as it spread westwards from Aeschylus, to Shakespeare, to Ibsen. My goal then, if my project was to reach fulfilment, was to expose myself to the great rôles created by these dramatists as they peered at life: and in their examination revealed its flaws, and in their revelation induced a change in our imagination.

Have not nations a project? Are there not goals to be reached in spite of the obduracy of human nature to admit the necessity of change? I think we have arrived at the moment in time when my land must make up its mind as to what its project is. At such a moment it is good to remind ourselves with, I hope, a becoming humility that there have been others before us who have experienced life most profoundly, and faced it and themselves with a serene imagination; and have enriched our lives by the goals (if only temporary because life itself is in continuous motion), by the signposts they have offered us.

A Bedside Book such as this might remind us of our temporary condition as life moves onwards. It might contain a modest suggestion that perhaps as our friends have misunderstood us, we have misunderstood ourselves.

A Bedside Book is no place for trumpets: only the suggested whisper that if one were to live it might be fruitful to aim like Montrose, and if death were to be our companion we might share the serenity of David Hume. I have found my countrymen deeply moving in their practice of life, and I hope that a little of that may be found by others.

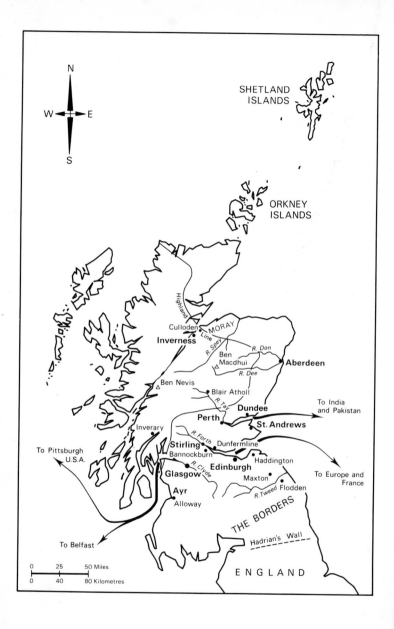

The Line

The Scots spoke Gaelic and originally came from the north of Ireland by way of the Hebrides. Their hostility prompted the Romans who were in occupation of England to build a wall so that the country between Hadrian's Wall and the Shetland Isles became known as Scotland. The east of the country is bounded by the North Sea, while on the west there lies the Atlantic Ocean. The population of this land has never exceeded six million.

Some time around the fifth century Christianity came to the country directly from Ireland, and by drift from the south. The religious establishment was Catholic, and discourse was in Latin.

The coronation of Charlemagne in Rome on Christmas Day in the year 800 not merely put an end to the Empire, but left the evolving nations of Europe with frontiers that had been established by Rome. For centuries there followed a struggle for power within these nations as families sought supremacy, and between nations as ambitions grew or security demanded. Scotland had more than its share of such families as the broken nature of the country and bad communications encouraged a multiplicity of groups, or clans as they ultimately came to be known. Scotland had one neighbour, England. Both from within and without there was matter for difference and war.

There was also a concern for other things . . .

About the year 1264 Johannes Duns Scotus was born in the Border village of Maxton. Little is known of him except that he provided the Franciscan order of the Middle Ages with an alternative theology to Thomism. There are three reasons why he should be remembered: he held that there was a principle of individuation irrespective of notions of matter and form; that the

13

Incarnation was not dependent on the Fall; and in spite of being known in his day as Dr Subtilis, provided the English with the word 'dunce'. He wrote in Latin, and died in Cologne about the year 1308, just six years before Bannockburn, the first great battle between the neighbours.

Many centuries later, the triumph of Bannockburn was cele-brated by Burns:

Scots, Wha Hae

Scots, wha hae wi' Wallace bled,
Scots, wham Bruce has aften led,
Welcome to your gory bed
  Or to victorie!

Now's the day, and now's the hour:
See the front o' battle lour,
See approach proud Edward's power—
  Chains and slaverie!

Wha will be a traitor knave?
Wha can fill a coward's grave?
Wha sae base as be a slave?—
  Let him turn, and flee!

Wha for Scotland's King and Law
Feedom's sword will strongly draw,
Freeman stand, or freeman fa',
  Let him follow me!

By Oppression's woes and pains,
By your sons in servile chains,
We will drain our dearest veins
  But they shall be free!

Lay the proud usurpers low!
Tyrants fall in every foe!
Liberty's in every blow!
    Let us do, or die!

Robert Burns, from THE OXFORD BOOK OF
SCOTTISH VERSE

Six years after Bannockburn a hundred men met on the east coast to give precision to their notions of liberty. This has become known as The Declaration of Arbroath:

TO the Most Holy Father in Christ and Lord, the Lord John, by divine providence Supreme Pontiff of the Holy Roman and Universal Church, his humble and devout sons Duncan, Earl of Fife, Thomas Randolph, Earl of Moray, Lord of Man and of Annandale, Patrick Dunbar, Earl of March, Malise, Earl of Strathearn, Malcolm, Earl of Lennox, William, Earl of Ross, Magnus, Earl of Caithness and Orkney, and William, Earl of Sutherland; Walter, Stewart of Scotland, William Soules, Butler of Scotland, James, Lord of Douglas, Roger Mowbray, David, Lord of Brechin, David Graham, Ingram Umfraville, John Menteith, guardian of the earldom of Menteith, Alexander Fraser, Gilbert Hay, Constable of Scotland, Robert Keith, Marischal of Scotland, Henry St. Clair, John Graham, David Lindsay, William Oliphant, Patrick Graham, John Fenton, William Abernethy, David Wemyss, William Mushet, Fergus of Ardrossan, Eustace Maxwell, William Ramsay, William Mowat, Alan Murray, Donald Campbell, John Cameron, Reginald Cheyne, Alexander Seton, Andrew Leslie, and Alexander Straiton, and the other barons and freeholders and the whole community of the realm of Scotland send all manner of filial reverence, with devout kisses of his blessed feet.

15

Most Holy Father and Lord, we know and from the chronicles and books of the ancients we find that among other famous nations our own, the Scots, has been graced with widespread renown. They journeyed from Greater Scythia by way of the Tyrrhenian Sea and the Pillars of Hercules, and dwelt for a long course of time in Spain among the most savage tribes, but nowhere could they be subdued by any race, however barbarous. Thence they came, twelve hundred years after the people of Israel crossed the Red Sea, to their home in the west where they still live today. The Britons they first drove out, the Picts they utterly destroyed, and, even though very often assailed by the Norwegians, the Danes and the English, they took possession of that home with many victories and untold efforts; and, as the historians of old time bear witness, they have held it free of all bondage ever since. In their kingdom there have reigned one hundred and thirteen kings of their own royal stock, the line unbroken by a single foreigner.

The high qualities and deserts of these people, were they not otherwise manifest, gain glory enough from this: that the King of kings and Lord of lords, our Lord Jesus Christ, after His Passion and Resurrection, called them, even though settled in the uttermost parts of the earth, almost the first to His most holy faith. Nor would He have them confirmed in that faith by merely anyone but by the first of His Apostles by calling—though second or third in rank—the most gentle Saint Andrew, the Blessed Peter's brother, and desired him to keep them under his protection as their patron for ever.

The Most Holy Fathers your predecessors gave careful heed to these things and bestowed many favours and numerous privileges on this same kingdom and people, as being the special charge of the Blessed Peter's brother. Thus our nation under their protection did indeed live in freedom and peace up to the time when that mighty prince the King of the English, Edward, the father of the one who reigns today, when our kingdom had no head and our people harboured no malice or treachery and were then unused to wars or invasions, came in the guise of a friend and ally to harass them as an enemy. The deeds of cruelty, massacre, violence, pillage, arson, imprisoning prelates, burning down monasteries, robbing and killing monks and nuns, and yet other outrages without number which he committed against our people, sparing neither age nor sex, religion nor rank, no one could describe nor fully imagine unless he had seen them with his own eyes.

But from these countless evils we have been set free, by the help of Him who though He afflicts yet heals and restores, by our most tireless Prince, King and Lord, the Lord Robert. He, that his people and his heritage might be delivered out of the hands of our enemies, met toil and fatigue, hunger and peril, like another Maccabaeus or Joshua, and bore them cheerfully. Him, too, divine providence, his right of succession according to our laws and customs which we shall maintain to the death, and the due consent and assent of us all have made our Prince and King. To him, as to the man by whom salvation has been wrought unto our people, we are bound both by law and by his merits that our freedom may be still maintained, and by him, come what may, we mean to stand.

Yet if he should give up what he has begun, and agree to make us or our kingdom subject to the King of England or the English, we should exert ourselves at once to drive him out as our enemy and a subverter of his own rights and ours, and make some other man who was well able to defend us our King; for, as long as but a hundred of us remain alive, never will we on any conditions be brought under English rule. It is in truth not for glory, nor riches, nor honours that we are fighting, but for freedom—for that alone, which no honest man gives up but with life itself.

Therefore it is, Reverend Father and Lord, that we beseech your Holiness with our most earnest prayers and suppliant hearts, inasmuch as you will in your sincerity and goodness consider all this, that, since with Him Whose vice-gerent on earth you are there is neither weighing nor distinction of Jew and Greek,

Scotsman or Englishman, you will look with the eyes of a father on the troubles and privations brought by the English upon us and upon the Church of God. May it please you to admonish and exhort the King of the English, who ought to be satisfied with what belongs to him since England used once to be enough for seven kings or more, to leave us Scots in peace, who live in this poor little Scotland, beyond which there is no dwelling-place at all, and covet nothing but our own. We are sincerely willing to do anything for him, having regard to our condition, that we can, to win peace for ourselves.

This truly concerns you, Holy Father, since you see the savagery of the heathen raging against the Christians, as the sins of Christians have indeed deserved, and the frontiers of Christendom being pressed inward every day; and how much it will tarnish your Holiness's memory if (which God forbid) the Church suffers eclipse or scandal in any branch of it during your time, you must perceive. Then rouse the Christian princes who for false reasons pretend that they cannot go to the help of the Holy Land because of wars they have on hand with their neighbours. The real reason that prevents them is that in making war on their smaller neighbours they find quicker profit and weaker resistance. But how cheerfully our Lord the King and we too would go there if the King of the English would leave us in peace, He from Whom nothing is hidden well knows; and we profess and declare it to you as the Vicar of Christ and to all Christendom.

But if your Holiness puts too much faith in the tales the English tell and will not give sincere belief to all this, nor refrain from favouring them to our prejudice, then the slaughter of bodies, the perdition of souls, and all the other misfortunes that will follow, inflicted by them on us and by us on them, will, we believe, be surely laid by the Most High to your charge.

To conclude, we are and shall ever be, as far as duty calls us, ready to do your will in all things, as obedient sons to you as His Vicar; and to Him as the Supreme King and Judge, we commit the maintenance of our cause, casting our cares upon Him and firmly trusting that He will inspire us with courage and bring our enemies to nought.

May the Most High preserve you to His Holy Church in holiness and health and grant you length of days.

Given at the monastery of Arbroath in Scotland on the sixth day of the month of April in the year of grace thirteen hundred and twenty and the fifteenth year of the reign of our King aforesaid.

THE DECLARATION OF ARBROATH, 1320

Towards the end of the eleventh century in France, there developed in Provence a unique synthesis of structural sensibility and refinement together with a delicate exploration of courtly love and chivalry. The structure made little impression on the rough habits of the Scottish clans (or in England for that matter), but it did mark the first great move away from Latin (the vulgate) towards a native language (the vernacular). The Borders were nearest to the influence and there was the richest collection of ballads, sometimes with a gruesome courtliness:

The Twa Corbies

As I was walking all alane,
I heard twa corbies making a mane;
The tane unto the t'other say,
'Where sall we gang and dine to-day?'

'In behint yon auld fail dyke,
I wot there lies a new slain knight;
And naebody kens that he lies there,
But his hawk, his hound, and lady fair.

19

'His hound is to the hunting gane,
His hawk to fetch the wild-fowl hame,
His lady's ta'en another mate,
So we may mak our dinner sweet.

'Ye'll sit on his white hause-bane,
And I'll pike out his bonny blue een;
Wi ae lock o his gowden hair
We'll theek our nest when it grows bare.

'Mony a one for him makes mane,
But nane sall ken where he is gane;
Oer his white banes, when they are bare,
The wind sall blaw for evermair.'

Anon, from THE OXFORD BOOK OF SCOTTISH VERSE

*Petrarch in Italy, Chaucer and Wyatt in England, Dunbar and
Henryson in Scotland rejoiced not only in the new kind of
language but in a newly discovered range of subjects, the classical
myths and Nature. Even a monarch projected his gracious
thoughts:*

Heigh in the hevynnis figure circulere
   The rody sterres twynklyng as the fyre;
And, in Aquary, Citherea the clere
Rynsid hir tressis like the goldin wyre,
   That late tofore, in fair and fresche atyre,
Through Capricorn heved hir hornis bright;
North northward approchit the mydnyght:

Quhen as I lay in bed allone waking,
    New partit out of slepe a lyte tofore,
Fell me to mynd of many divers thing,
    Off this and that; can I noght say quharfore,
    Bot slepe for craft in erth myght I no more;
For quhich as tho coude I no better wyle,
Bot toke a boke to rede apon a quhile:

from 'The Kingis Quair', James I, 1394–1437,
THE OXFORD BOOK OF SCOTTISH VERSE

Repetition can never be guaranteed. Almost two hundred years after the triumph of Bannockburn, the same neighbour in 1513 inflicted the despair of Flodden. This time Jean Elliot had a word for it.

The Flowers of the Forest

I've heard the lilting at our yowe-milking,
    Lasses a-lilting before the dawn o' day;
But now they are moaning on ilka green loaning:
    'The Flowers of the Forest are a' wede away.'

At buchts, in the morning, nae blythe lads are scorning;
    The lasses are lonely, and dowie, and wae;
Nae daffin', nae gabbin', but sighing and sabbing:
    Ilk ane lifts her leglen, and hies her away.

In hairst, at the shearing, nae youths now are jeering,
    The bandsters are lyart, and runkled and grey;
At fair or at preaching, nae wooing, nae fleeching:
    The Flowers of the Forest are a' wede away.

At e'en, in the gloaming, nae swankies are roaming
　'Bout stacks wi' the lasses at bogle to play,
But ilk ane sits drearie, lamenting her dearie:
　The Flowers of the Forest are a' wede away.

Dule and wae for the order sent our lads to the Border;
　The English, for ance, by guile wan the day;
The Flowers of the Forest, that foucht aye the foremost,
　The prime o' our land, are cauld in the clay.

We'll hear nae mair lilting at our yowe-milking,
　Women and bairns are heartless and wae;
Sighing and moaning on ilka green loaning:
　'The Flowers of the Forest are a' wede away.'

Jean Elliot, 1727–1805, from THE OXFORD BOOK
OF SCOTTISH VERSE

Five years after Flodden in 1518, Luther nailed his 95 theses to the Schlosskirche at Wittenberg. About 1514 John Knox was born in Haddington. Reform in religion and society was on the way.

The Scottish Clan System

The relationship of clanship to feudalism, which has been much misunderstood, is also one which, if clanship is to take its proper share in the Scotland of the future, requires to be more clearly appreciated. Indeed, but for Feudalism, we should have had no Clans to-day, probably no 'clans' at all, as we Scotsmen understand the term.

It was just because the Feudo-Celtic system proved the ideal

MacDonell of Glengarry in full insignia

machinery for perpetuating the 'functions of the tribal leader' and the *spirit of the tribe*, that 'clanship' developed in Scotland instead of tribalism being destroyed as in most other lands.

It is this intensity of tribe-affection for even a poor and barren inheritance, which is immediately evident on entering Scotland. This is of the essence of Clanship—the tribe and *its* soil—but with the subdivision into still more individual but equally sacred holdings. Not only in secular, but likewise in sacred affairs, the intense appreciation of continuance and heredity is evinced in the hereditary character of the Celtic Church, with its married priesthood and lines of hereditary Abbots. It is this all-pervading sense of racial continuity, running through all our institutions, which gives the key to Scottish civilisation. Moreover, it is the subsistence of that continuity as a still vital force that strikes an appeal to the deepest instincts of human nature, and gives our institutions their unfailing interest, charm, or, if you will, 'romance'—not only to Scots themselves, but to all who pause to consider what 'Scotland' stands for in the story of the Nations.

Sir Thomas Innes of Learney, TARTANS OF THE CLANS
AND FAMILIES OF SCOTLAND

For centuries while England had only two, Scotland had four universities, at St Andrews, Glasgow, Edinburgh and Aberdeen, all founded by the sixteenth century. Their links with European universities, especially Bologna and Paris was close. In the sixteenth century John Knox, aware that the Reformation had destroyed the classical mode of education, placed before the nation the ideal of 'a school in every parish'.

John Knox

That scything wind has cut the rich corn down—
the satin shades of France spin idly by—
the bells are jangled in St. Andrew's town—
a thunderous God tolls from a northern sky.
He pulls the clouds like bandages awry.
See how the harlot bleeds below her crown.
This lightning stabs her in the heaving thigh—
such siege is deadly for dallying gown.

A peasant's scythe rings churchbells from the stone.
From this harsh battle let the sweet birds fly,
surprised by fields, now barren of their corn.
(Invent, bright friends, theology, or die.)
The shearing naked absolute blade has torn
through false French roses to her foreign cry.

Iain Crichton Smith, from THE OXFORD BOOK OF
SCOTTISH VERSE

*　　*　　*

Information in the evening as the day closes opens the mind to
another kind of reflection. It may be, for instance, that away from
the professional study of books the explanation of how a letter
came to be written may tell us in an acceptable manner how
history moves, and induce that feeling of the past which we can
embrace with some grace. And grace, however we understand it,
is something we ascribe to Mary of Scotland.

This letter was completed by Mary, Queen of Scots, at two
o'clock in the morning on Wednesday 8th February 1587, six

25

hours before she was to mount the scaffold at Fotheringay Castle. It is addressed to Henri III, King of France, younger brother of her first husband, Francis II, who had died of an ear-infection in 1559 at the age of 17.

Mary's short reign in Scotland, from 1561 to 1567, was at first characterized by stable policy and government, in spite of clashes with the protestant reformer, John Knox, over her right to worship according to her Catholic beliefs. But subsequently her emotional involvements, with Henry Stuart, Lord Darnley, and later with James Hepburn, Earl of Bothwell, led to the breakdown of this stability, to the rebellion of the Protestant lords, and to Mary's abdication and flight into England.

Elizabeth, the English Queen, was faced with a dilemma. Instinctively she desired to support her cousin Mary against the Scottish Reformers, seeing their actions as striking at the roots of all monarchy. On the other hand Mary, dowager Queen of France, and Queen of Scots, was also heiress to the English throne. In fact, to Catholics throughout Europe, Mary was rightful Queen of England, since Elizabeth herself was the illegitimate daughter of Henry VIII. To maintain her own position at the head of the English state, Elizabeth could not afford to allow Mary to remain at liberty.

None the less, throughout the eighteen years of her imprisonment, Mary symbolized the aspirations not only of the English Catholics hoping for the restoration of their country to Catholicism but also of the rival Catholic Kings of France and Spain, who each hoped, by placing her on the English throne, to bring England within his own sphere of political and diplomatic influence. Directly or indirectly, Mary was involved in plots against the English Queen, in plans for Catholic risings in England, and in diplomatic intrigues on the continent. By the Ridolfi plot (1571), the Throckmorton plot (1583), and the Babington conspiracy (1586), all involving the threat of foreign invasion, the English government was persuaded that, to ensure the political stability of England, Mary could not be allowed to live. Eventually Elizabeth, although disturbed at the thought of executing her cousin, a monarch in her own right, agreed.

While the English government insisted that the death of Mary was purely a political matter, she herself, as she conveys in this her last letter, believed she was dying a religious martyr. But what concerned her equally when she wrote to the King of France, with whom she had corresponded regularly while in captivity, was the well-being of her household servants after her execution. In effect, few of these servants returned to their native lands of France and Scotland, and not until late in 1587 was Bourgoing, Mary's physician, able to make his way to France and give his report to Henri III, presumably delivering this letter at the same time. It was, however, left to Philip II of Spain to authorize, through his ambassador Bernardino Mendoza, the payment of wages and pensions to Mary's servants.

The letter itself no doubt remained in the French royal archives, and later, at some unknown date, was given to the Scots College in Paris, a Catholic seminary for Scottish priests, probably as a relic of the martyred Queen. There it remained until the French Revolution, when the College was dissolved, and its archives dispersed. It passed into the hands of the Chevalier d'Hervilly, and eventually into the celebrated collection of autographs formed by Alfred Morrison. In 1918 the letter was purchased by a group of subscribers and presented to the Scottish Nation through the National Art-Collections Fund.

Queen of Scotland
8 Feb. 1587

Royal brother, having by God's will, for my sins I think, thrown myself into the power of the Queen my cousin, at whose hands I have suffered much for almost twenty years, I have finally been condemned to death by her and her Estates. I have asked for my papers, which they have taken away, in order that I might make my will, but I have been unable to recover anything of use to me, or even get leave either to make my will freely or to have my body conveyed after my death, as I would wish, to your kingdom where I had the honour to be queen, your sister and old ally.

Tonight, after dinner, I have been advised of my sentence: I am to be executed like a criminal at eight in the morning. I have not had time to give you a full account of everything that has happened, but if you will listen to my doctor and my other unfortunate servants, you will learn the truth, and how, thanks be to God, I scorn death and vow that I meet it innocent of any crime, even if I were their subject. The Catholic faith and the assertion of my God-given right to the English crown are the two issues on which I am condemned, and yet I am not allowed to say that it is for the Catholic religion that I die, but for fear of interference with theirs. The proof of this is that they have taken away my chaplain, and, although he is in the building, I have not been able to get permission for him to come and hear my confession and give me the Last Sacrament, while they have been most insistent that I receive the consolation and instruction of their minister, brought here for that purpose. The bearer of this letter and his companions, most of them your subjects, will testify to my conduct at my last hour. It remains for me to beg Your Most Christian Majesty, my brother-in-law and old ally, who have always protested your love for me, to give proof now of your goodness on all these points: firstly by charity, in paying my unfortunate servants the wages due them—this is a burden on my conscience that only you can relieve: further, by having prayers offered to God for a queen who has borne the title Most Christian, and who dies a Catholic, stripped of all her possessions. As for my son, I commend him to you in so far as he deserves, for I cannot answer for him. I have taken the liberty of sending you two precious stones, talismans against illness, trusting that you will enjoy good health and a long and happy life. Accept them from your loving sister-in-law, who, as she dies, bears witness of her warm feeling for you. Again I commend my servants to you. Give instructions, if it please you, that for my soul's sake part of what you owe me should be paid, and that for the sake of Jesus Christ, to whom I shall pray for you tomorrow as I die, I be left enough to found a memorial mass and give the customary alms.

Wednesday, at two in the morning.
Your most loving and most true sister,

MARY R.

To the Most Christian King, my brother and old ally.

The last letter of Mary Queen of Scots

*   *   *

A diversion—the entry of science into the nation.

The classical world-view, held by all countries of Europe until Copernicus, was stated by Socrates. This was that the individual was the centre of the world and the entire world centred in him, and this self-knowledge was the knowledge of God. In the sixteenth century Copernicus proposed that far from being the centre of the world, the earth moved round the sun, and that the world view should move from anthropocentric to heliocentric. Galileo and Newton followed Copernicus in formulating new insights into the nature of time and space. But the measurements and numbers were vast.

John Napier (1550–1617), laird of Merchiston, discovered logarithms. Napier was an eccentric whose eccentricity has been continually emphasised to the detriment of his insight and inventiveness. The advantages of a table of logarithms are that by its employment multiplication and division can be performed by simple addition and subtraction, the extraction of the roots of numbers by division, and the raising of them to any power by multiplication. By these simple processes the most complicated problems in astronomy, navigation and the cognate sciences (the new sciences) can be solved by an easy and certain method which was also exact. Napier was a great originator, and the first Scotsman to make a contribution of outstanding value through mathematics to the modern scientific view.

James Corss, a Glaswegian, commented in 1662:

I have oftentimes lamented with myself to see so many Learned Mathematicians to arise in sundry parts of the world, and so few to appear in our Native Country. In other things we are parallel with (I shall not say in a superlative degree far above) other Nations; but in Arts and Sciences Mathematical, all exceed us. And had not that thrice Noble and Illustrious Lord, viz John Lord Nepper, Baron of Merchiston, &c. preserved the honour of our Nation by his admirable and more than mortal invention of Logarithms, we should have been buried in oblivion, in the memories of Forraign Nations.

James Corss, URANOSCOPIA: THE CONTEMPLATION
OF THE HEAVENS IN A PERPETUAL SPECULUM, OR
GENERAL PROGNOSTICATION FOR EVER

*   *   *

The seventeenth century in Scotland as in Europe is the dark century, and for two great reasons. The first lay in the implications of Luther and Calvin not merely for a Catholic theology but for a society based on hierarchy. Equality—albeit before God—is on the horizon. But the second reason is more refined. The new insights into time and space evoked a new kind of instrumentation which laid the ground for the industrial revolution. For the verification of these insights, experiments were needed, and the instruments to measure them; telescopes to view the heavens, and microscopes to observe minute detail. A completely new dimension of experience, unknown to the Greeks, was slowly emerging in Europe—the application of scientific

30

theory to practice and everyday use. It was a preoccupation with which Scotland was to be greatly concerned. But in the seventeenth century, it was a paradox that European thinkers like Napier, Bacon, Locke and Descartes should be engaged in the refinements of scientific thought while the people themselves were embroiled in the worst kind of wars—wars about the nature of their way of life, civil wars.

Scotland's greatest soldier seized upon a point of law, the lawful succession of the monarchy, and accomplished feats of generalship to rival a Marlborough, or modern commanders like Lawrence and Rommel. After James had succeeded Elizabeth, and his son had in turn come to the throne, anxious to assert the Catholic nature of the monarchy, the situation was open to strife. Montrose was not concerned with theology, but greatly interested in legality and succession. He found himself fighting against his own countrymen—very much in a minority. Yet he inspired a motley collection of undisciplined clansmen to astonishing military feats.

The Highland Line in the Scottish mainland, though variously determined at times by political needs, has been clearly fixed by nature. The main battlement of the hills runs with a north-easterly slant from Argyll through the Lennox, and then turns northward so as to enclose the wide carselands of Tay. Beyond lie the tangled wildernesses stretching with scarcely a break to Cape Wrath; east and south are the Lowlands proper—on the east around Don and Dee and the Forfarshire Esks: on the south around Forth and Clyde, and embracing the hills of Tweed and Galloway. Scotland had thus two borderlands—the famous line of march with England, and the line, historically less notable but geographically clearer, which separated plain from hill, family from clan, and for centuries some semblance of civilization from its stark opposite. The northern Border may be defined in its more essential part as the southern portion of Dumbarton and Lennox, the shire of

Stirling, and the haughs of the Lower Tay. There for centuries the Lowlander looked out from his towns and castles to the blue mountains where lived his ancestral foes. Dwelling on a frontier makes a hardy race, and from this northern Border came famous men and sounding deeds. Drummonds, Murrays, Erskines, and Grahams were its chief families, but most notably the last. What the name of Scott was in the glens of Teviot, the name of Graham was in the valleys of Forth and Earn. Since the thirteenth century they had been the unofficial wardens of the northern marches.

The ancient nobility of Scotland does not show well on the page of history. The records of the great earldoms—Angus, Mar, Moray, Buchan—tell too often an unedifying tale of blood and treason, and, after the day of the Good Lord James, St Bride of Douglas might have wept for her children. But the family of Graham kept tolerably clean hands, and played an honourable part in the national history. Sir John the Graham was the trusted friend of Wallace, and fell gloriously at Falkirk. His successors fought in the later wars of independence, thrice inter-married with the royal blood, and gave Scotland her first primate. In 1451 the family attained the peerage. The third Lord Graham was made Earl of Montrose, when the short-lived Lindsay dukedom lapsed, and the new earl died with his king in the steel circle at Flodden. A successor fell at Pinkie; another became Chancellor and then Viceroy of Scotland when James the Sixth mounted the English throne. The Viceroy's son, the fourth earl, apart from a famous brawl in the High Street of Edinburgh, lived the quiet life of a county laird till, shortly before his death he, too, was appointed Chancellor. He was a noted sportsman, a great golfer, and a devotee of tobacco. His wife was Lady Margaret Ruthven, a daughter of the tragically-fated house of Gowrie, who bore him six children, and died when her only son was in his sixth year. The family was reasonably rich as the times went, for the home-keeping Earl John had conserved his estate. They owned broad lands in Stirling, Perth, and Angus, and wielded the influence which the chief of a house possesses over its numerous cadets.

32

They had three principal dwellings—the tower of Mugdock in Strathblane; the fine castle of Kincardine in Perthshire, where the Ochils slope to the Earn; and the house of Old Montrose, which Robert Bruce had given to a Graham as the price of Cardross on Clyde.

The Marquis of Montrose

James Graham, the only son of the fourth earl and Margaret Ruthven, was born in the year 1612, probably in the month of October—according to tradition in the town of Montrose. The piety of opponents has surrounded his birth with omens; his mother is said, with the hereditary Ruthven love of necromancy, to have consulted witches, and his father to have observed to a neighbour that this child would trouble all Scotland. Like Cromwell, he was the only boy in a family of girls. Of his five sisters, the two eldest were married young—Lilias to Sir John Colquhoun of Luss, and Margaret to a wise man of forty, the first Lord Napier of Merchiston. Their houses were open to him when he tired of catching trout in the little water of Ruthven, or wearing out horseshoes on the Ochils, an occupation to which the extant bills of the Aberuthven blacksmith testify. There was much in the way of adventure to be had at Rossdhu, Lady Lilias's new dwelling, and there the boy may have learned, from practising on the roebuck and wild goats of Lochlomondside, the skill which made him in after years a noted marksman.

At the age of twelve Lord Graham was entrusted to a certain William Forrett, master of arts, to be prepared for the college of Glasgow. Thither he journeyed with a valet, two pages in scarlet, a quantity of linen and plate, a selection from his father's library, and his favourite white pony. He lived in the house of Sir George Elphinstone of Blythswood, the Lord Justice Clerk; it stood near the Townhead, and may have been one of the old manses of the canons of the Cathedral. The avenues to learning must have been gently graded, for he retained a happy memory of those Glasgow days and of Master Forrett, who in later years became the tutor of his sons. He seems to have read in Xenophon and Seneca, and an English translation of Tasso; but his favourite book, then and long afterwards, was Raleigh's *History of the World*, the splendid folio of the first edition.

In the second year of Glasgow study the old earl died, and Lord Graham posted back to Kincardine, arriving two days before the end. Thither came the whole race of Grahams for the funeral ceremonies, which lasted the better part of three weeks. Prodigious quantities of meat and drink were consumed, for each neighbour and kinsman brought his contribution in kind—partridges and plovers from Lord Stormont, moorfowl from Lawers, a great hind from Glenorchy—the details are still extant, with the values of woodcock and wild geese, capercailzie and ptarmigan, meticulously set down. If such mourning had its drawbacks, at any rate it introduced the new head of the family to those of his name and race. He did not return to Glasgow (though five years later he showed his affection for the place by making a donation to the building of the new college library), and presently was entered at St. Salvator's College, St. Andrews, of which one of his forbears had been a founder. Master Forrett brought his possessions from Glasgow, and the laird of Inchbrakie bestowed these valuable items, the books, in a proper cabinet.

We have ample documents to illustrate his St. Andrews' days. The university, the oldest and then the most famous in Scotland, had among its alumni in the first half of the seventeenth century men so diverse as Montrose and Argyll and Rothes, Mr. Donald Cargill and Sir George Mackenzie. His secretary was a Mr. John Lambie, and Mr. Lambie's accounts reveal the academic life in those days of a gentleman-commoner. In sport his tastes were catholic. He golfed, like James Melville a century before, and paid five shillings Scots for each golf ball. His rooms at St. Salvator's were hung round with bows, and in his second year he won the silver medal for archery, which to the end of his college course he held against all comers. Argyll, who was some years his senior, had carried off the same trophy. He was an admirable horseman, and he seems to have hunted regularly; it is recorded in the accounts that after a day with hounds his horse was given a pint of ale. He was fond of hawking, and he went regularly to Cupar races, handing over, according to the excellent statute of 1621, his winnings beyond one hundred marks to the local kirk session for the relief of the poor. His chief friends of his own order seem to have been Wigton, Lindsay of the Byres, Kinghorn, Sinclair,

Sutherland, and Colville, and he varied his residence at St. Andrews with visits to his brother-in-law (the hills of Rossdhu, complains his steward, wore the boots off his feet), the cadet gentry of his name, and Cumbernauld, Glamis, Kinnaird, Balcarres, and the other country-houses of his friends. In October 1628 he gave a great house-warming at Kincardine, which lasted for three days. In the March following he visited Edinburgh, where he appeared in gilt spurs and a new sword, and was lent the Chancellor's carriage. The picture which has come down to us of the undergraduate is that of a boy happy and well-dowered, popular with all, eager to squeeze the juice from the many fruits of life. Nor was he above youthful disasters. When his sister Dorothea married Sir James Rollo, there was huge feasting in Edinburgh and Fife, and the young earl returned to college only to fall sick. Two doctors were summoned, who charged enormous fees, and prescribed a rest cure—strict diet, and no amusements but cards and chess. The barber shore away his long brown curls, and "James Pett's dochter" attended to the invalid's food. The régime seems high feeding for what was probably an attack of indigestion—trout, pigeons, capons, "drapped eggs," calf's-foot jelly, grouse (out of season), washed down by "liquorice, whey, possets, ale-berry, and claret."

From the accounts preserved we can trace something of his progress in learning. He began to study Greek, and continued his reading in the Latin classics, his favourites now being Cæsar and Lucan, in his copies of which he made notes. He can never have been an exact scholar, and it is probable that the wide knowledge of classical literature which he showed later was largely acquired from translations. For it was the day of great translators, and at St. Andrews he had at his service North's *Plutarch*, Philemon Holland's *Livy* and *Suetonius*, Thomas Heywood's *Sallust*, and the *Tacitus* of Sir Henry Savile and Richard Grenewey. Nor did he neglect romances, and he made his first essays in poetry. To this stage may belong the lines ascribed to him by family tradition, in which the ambitious boy writes his own version of a popular

36

contemporary conceit; but he does not end, like the other versions, on a note of pious quietism:

> "I would be high; but that the cedar tree
> Is blustered down whilst smaller shrubs go free.
> I would be low; but that the lowly grass
> Is trampled down by each unworthy ass.
> For to be high, my means they will not doe;
> And to be low my mind it will not bow.
> O Heavens! O Fate! when will you once agree
> To reconcile my means, my mind, and me?"

John Buchan, MONTROSE

Scotland at war with itself: Argyll and Montrose—the Campaign of Inverlochy.

> Through the land of my fathers the Campbells have come,
> The flames of their foray enveloped my home;
> Broad Keppoch in ruin is left to deplore,
> And my country is waste from the hill to the shore.
> Be it so! By St. Mary, there's comfort in store!
>
> Though the braes of Lochaber a desert be made,
> And Glen Roy may be lost to the plough and the spade,
> Though the bones of my kindred, unhonoured, unurned,
> Mark the desolate path where the Campbells have burned—
> Be it so! From that foray they never returned.

Ian Lom Macdonald *(Mark Napier's translation)*

In seventeenth-century Scotland clan Campbell stood by itself as a separate race, almost a separate state, whose politics were determined by the whim of its ruling prince. Built upon the ruins of many little septs, it excelled in numbers and wealth every other Highland clan; indeed, if we except the Gordons, it surpassed in importance all the rest put together. It was near enough to the Lowlands to have shared in such civilization as was going, including the new theology. Craftsmen had been brought to Inveraray from the Ayr and Renfrew burghs, schools had been

37

established, and of a Sunday the townsfolk could listen to notable preachers of the Word. On the other hand, its territory was a compact block, well guarded on all sides from its neighbours, so that it enjoyed the peace and confidence of a separate people. With its immense sea-coast its doors were open to the wider world, and the Campbell gentry acquired at foreign universities and in foreign wars a training which few landward gentlemen could boast; while Flemish velvets and the silks and wines of France came more readily and cheaply to its little towns than to the burghers of Perth or Edinburgh. The country, though less fertile than the Lowlands, was a champaign compared to Lochaber or Kintail. Thousands of black cattle flourished on its juicy hill pastures, and farms and shielings were thick along the pleasant glens that sloped to Loch Fyne and Loch Awe. In the town of Inveraray the clan had its natural capital, and from Inveraray ran the Lowland road through Cowal and Dumbarton for such as preferred a land journey. Compared with other clans, the Campbells were prosperous and civilized; they did not live from hand to mouth like the rest, nor did each winter find them at the brink of starvation; yet they still retained the martial spirit of the Gael, and could put into the field the most formidable of Highland levies. Accordingly, by their neighbours they were both detested and feared. They had eaten up the little peoples of Benderloch and Morvern, and their long arm was stretching north and east into Lochaber and Strathtay. Every Maclean and Stewart who could see the hills of Lorn from his doorstep had uneasy thoughts about his own barren acres. The Campbells had a knack of winning by bow and spear, and then holding for all time by seal and parchment.

Not without reason Argyll boasted that his land was impregnable, for strategically it had every advantage. On the eastern side, where it looked to the Lowlands, there were the castles of Roseneath and Dunoon to keep ward, and deep sea-lochs to check the invader. Besides, the Lowlands and Argyll were always at peace. South and west lay the sea, and the Campbells had what little navy existed at the time in Scotland. The Macleans in Mull were too small and broken to take the offensive, and in any case it was a long way from the coast at Knapdale to the heart of Inveraray. North and east lay a land of high mountains and difficult passes, where no man could travel save by permission of the sovereign lord. Moreover, the Campbells of Lochow and Glenorchy had flung their tentacles over Breadalbane, and held the marches around the headwaters of Tay. There might be a raid of Macgregors or Maclarens on the east, or a foray from Appin on Loch Etive side, but not even the king and his army could get much beyond the gates. "It is a far cry to Lochow," so ran the Campbell owercome, and it was a farther cry to Inveraray.

Montrose, when he assented to Alasdair's wishes, resolved to strike straight at the enemy's heart. He would wage war not in the outskirts, but in the citadel. From Blair there was little choice of roads. To go due west by Rannoch and the springs of Etive would mean a march among friendly clans, but a few score Campbells could hold the narrows of Loch Etive or the Pass of Brander against the strongest army. The Lowland road by Dumbarton and Loch Lomond was out of the question, for it meant a dangerous proximity to the Covenanting westlands and the difficult pass of Glencroe. But midway through Breadalbane ran a possible route, among wild glens and trackless bogs, which at this winter season would be deep in snow. This was the old raiding road out of Lorn, and Argyll flattered himself that his clan alone had the keys of it. But with Montrose were men who had made many a midnight foray into the Campbell domain, and who knew every corrie and moss as well as any son of Diarmaid. A Glencoe man, Angus MacAlain Dubh, was the chief guide, and he promised Montrose that his army should live well on the country, "if tight houses, fat cattle, and clear water will suffice." Accordingly, with Airlie and the Ogilvys and his eldest boy, Lord Graham, as his Lowland staff, the king's lieutenant ordered the march to the west. The army travelled in three divisions: the Ulstermen under Alasdair in three regiments, commanded respectively by James Macdonnell, Ranald Og Macdonnell, and Magnus O'Cahan; the western clans, Macdonalds, Camerons, Stewarts, and Macleans, under John of Moidart, Captain of Clanranald; the Atholl, Badenoch, and Aberdeenshire contingents, and the small Lowland force under the king's lieutenant himself. Montrose had now some 3,000 troops, drawn from every corner of Scotland. There were men from Orkney, from Uist, and from Skye; from the whole Highland mainland between Knoydart and Braemar; from Kintyre; from Angus and Moray and Buchan; from the villages of Forth, Earn, and Tay; even from Lothian, Galloway, and the distant Borders.

Montrose left Blair on or about the 11th day of December. The road was at first the same as that taken in the march to Tippermuir. The lands of the small and uncertain clan of Menzies were traversed, and the laird of Weem taken prisoner. Then westward by both shores of Loch Tay swept the advance, where the Macdougal settlers from Lorn suffered, till the confines of Breadalbane were reached and a country that owned Campbell sway. Up Glen Dochart they went, following much the same road as the present railway line to Oban, past Crianlarich and Tyndrum, and into the glens of Orchy. John of Moidart, with the western men, was sent on in advance, and did not rejoin the army till Kilmartin Glassary, far down in Argyll; his business was to collect food, and he brought in a thousand head of cattle. In Glen Dochart Montrose was joined by the local septs, the Macnabs and the Macgregors, and it was by a ruse of the former wily and resourceful clan that the difficult narrows of Loch Dochart were passed, and the island castle was surrendered. A Catholic priest was the meteorologist of the army, and he had promised them that the weather would hold, since the wind blew from the east; he proved right, for there was neither rain nor snow to hinder their speed.

It was partly a raid of vengeance, and behind them rose the flames of burning roof-trees. Presently Loch Awe lay before them under the leaden winter sky, and soon the little fortalices of the lochside lairds smoked to heaven. All fighting men who resisted were slain or driven to the high hills, every cot and clachan was set alight, and droves of maddened cattle attested the richness of the land and the profit of the invaders. It was Highland warfare of the old barbarous type, no worse and no better than that which Argyll had already carried to Lochaber and Badenoch and the braes of Angus.

Argyll was well served by his scouts, and to him at Edinburgh word was soon brought of Montrose's march to Breadalbane. He must have thought it a crazy venture. Now at last was his enemy delivered into his hands. No mortal army could cross the winter passes, even if it had the key, and the men of Glenorchy would wipe out the starving remnants at their leisure. Full of confidence he posted across Scotland to Inveraray. There he found that all was quiet. Rumours of a foray in Lorn were indeed rife, but the burghers of Inveraray, strong in their generations of peace, had no fear for themselves. Argyll saw to the defences of his castle, and called a great gathering of his clansmen to provide reinforcements, if such should be needed, for the Glenorchy and Breadalbane men, who by that time had assuredly made an end of Montrose.

Suddenly came the thunderbolt. Wild-eyed shepherds rushed into the streets with the cry that the Macdonalds were upon them. Quickly the tale grew. Montrose was not in Breadalbane or on the fringes of Lorn; he was at Loch Awe—nay, he was in the heart of Argyll itself. The chief waited no longer. He found a fishing-boat and, the wind being right, fled down Loch Fyne to the shelter of his castle of Roseneath. The same breeze that filled his sails brought the sound of Alasdair's pipes, and he was scarcely under way ere the van of the invaders came down Glen Shira. The miracle had happened, and the impregnable fortress had fallen. "We see," commented Mr. Robert Baillie piously, but obscurely, "there is no strength or refuge on earth against the Lord."

John Buchan, MONTROSE

From Montrose to his Mistress

My dear and only Love, I pray
   This noble World of thee,
Be govern'd by no other Sway
   But purest Monarchie.
For if Confusion have a Part,
   Which vertuous Souls abhore,
And hold a Synod in thy Heart,
   I'll never love thee more.

Like *Alexander* I will reign,
   And I will reign alone,
My Thoughts shall evermore disdain
   A Rival on my Throne.
He either fears his Fate too much,
   Or his Deserts are small,
That puts it not unto the Touch,
   To win or lose it all.

John Graham, Marquis of Montrose, from
THE OXFORD BOOK OF SCOTTISH VERSE

It was a gallant campaign but fruitless; a lukewarm king, diminishing resources inadequate against the increasing power of the establishment in Scotland and England. Montrose after a sojourn in Europe returned to Scotland where he was betrayed and incarcerated in Edinburgh Castle.

In prison

Presently he heard the drums beating to arms, and was told that the troops were assembling to prevent any attempt at a rescue. He laughed and cried: "What, am I still a terror to them? Let them look to themselves; my ghost will haunt them."

He was taken about two in the afternoon by the bailies down the High Street to the Mercat Cross, which stood between the

Tolbooth and the Tron Kirk—that dolorous road which Argyll and Wariston and James Guthrie were themselves to travel. He still wore the brave clothes in which he had confronted Parliament; nay, more, he had ribbons on his shoes and fine white gloves on his hands. James Fraser, who saw him, wrote: "He stept along the streets with so great state, and there appeared in his countenance so much beauty, majesty, and gravity as amazed the beholder, and many of his enemies did acknowledge him to be the bravest subject in the world, and in him a gallantry that braced all that crowd." Another eyewitness, John Nicoll, the notary public, thought him more like a bridegroom than a criminal. An Englishman among the spectators, a Commonwealth agent, wrote an account to his masters. "It is absolutely certain that he hath overcome more men by his death, in Scotland, than he would have done if he had lived. For I never saw a more sweeter carriage in a man in all my life."

The scaffold was a great four-square platform, breast-high, and on it a 30-foot gallows had been erected. On the platform stood the ministers, Mr. Robert Traill and Mr. Mungo Law, still bent on getting a word of confession or penitence. They were disappointed, for Montrose did not look at them. He was not allowed to address the mob, which surged up against the edge of the scaffold—a privilege hitherto granted to the meanest criminals; but he spoke apart to the magistrates and to a few of the nearer spectators. A boy called Robert Gordon sat by and took down his words in some kind of shorthand, and the crowd, with that decency which belongs to all simple folk, kept a reverent silence. The Estates were afraid lest he should attack the king and spoil their game, but he spoke no word of bitterness or reproach; rather—*splendide mendax*—he praised Charles's justice. It was the testament of a man conscious of his mortal frailty, but confident in the purity of his purpose and the mercy of his God.

"I am sorry if this manner of my end be scandalous to any good Christian here. Doth it not often happen to the righteous according to the way of the unrighteous? Doth not sometimes a just man perish in his righteousness, and a wicked man prosper in his wickedness and malice? They who know me should not disesteem me for this. Many greater than I have been dealt with in this kind. But I must not say but that all God's judgments are just, and this measure, for my private sins, I acknowledge to be just with God, and wholly submit myself to Him.

"But, in regard of man, I must say they are but instruments. God forgive them, and I forgive them. They have oppressed the poor and violently perverted judgment and justice, but He that is higher than they will reward them.

"What I did in this kingdom was in obedience to the most just commands of my sovereign, and in his defence, in the day of his distress, against those who rose up against him. I acknowledge nothing, but fear God and honour the king, according to the commandments of God and the just laws of Nature and nations. I have not sinned against man, but against God; and with Him there is mercy, which is the ground of my drawing near unto Him.

"It is objected against me by many, even good people, that I am under the censure of the Church. This is not my fault, seeing it is only for doing my duty, by obeying my prince's most just commands, for religion, his sacred person, and authority. Yet I am sorry they did excommunicate me; and in that which is according to God's laws, without wronging my conscience or allegiance, I desire to be relaxed. If they will not do it, I appeal to God, who is the righteous Judge of the world, and will, I hope, be my Judge and Saviour.

"It is spoken of me that I should blame the king. God forbid! For the late king, he lived a saint and died a martyr. I pray God I may end as he did. If ever I would wish my soul in another man's stead, it should be in his. For his Majesty now living, never any people, I believe, might be more happy in a king. His commandments to me were most just, and I obeyed them. He deals justly with all men. I pray God he be so dealt withal that he be not betrayed under trust, as his father was.

"I desire not to be mistaken, as if my carriage at this time, in relation to your ways, were stubborn. I do but follow the light of my conscience, my rule; which is seconded by the working of the Spirit of God that is within me. I thank Him I go to heaven with joy the way He paved for me. If He enable me against the fear of death, and furnish me with courage and confidence to embrace it even in its most ugly shape, let God be glorified in my end, though it were in my damnation. Yet I say not this out of any fear or mistrust, but out of my duty to God, and love to His people.

"I have no more to say, but that I desire your charity and prayers. I shall pray for you all. I leave my soul to God, my service to my prince, my goodwill to my friends, my love and charity to you all. And thus briefly I have exonerated my conscience."

There is a tradition that during the morning there had been

lowering thunder-clouds and flashes of lightning, but that as Montrose stood on the scaffold a burst of sunlight flooded the street. When he had finished speaking, he gave money to his executioner, and prayed silently for a little. His arms were pinioned, and he ascended the ladder with that stately carriage which had always marked him. His last words were: "God have mercy on this afflicted land!" Tears ran down the hangman's face as he pushed him off, and we are told that a great sob broke from the crowd. They had cause to sob, for that day there was done to death such a man as his country has not seen again.

According to the sentence, the body was cut down after three hours and the limbs distributed among the chief towns. The remains in Aberdeen must have caught the eye of Charles when he arrived a few weeks later. The trunk was buried beside the public gallows on the Boroughmuir. The head was placed on a spike on the west face of the Tolbooth, and eleven years later was taken down to make room for the head of Argyll.

There was to be another funeral besides that melancholy scene by lantern light among the marshes of the Boroughmuir. After the Restoration, one of Charles's first acts was to give public burial to the remains of his great captain. On January 4, 1661, the Scots Parliament resolved on "an honourable reparation for that horrid and monstrous barbarity in the person of the great Marquis of Montrose." The trunk was solemnly taken up from the Boroughmuir, and the limbs gathered from the several towns, a ceremony attended by "the honest people's loud and joyful acclamations." The remains, wrapped in fine linen in a noble coffin, lay in state in the Abbey Kirk of Holyrood from the 7th of January to the 11th of May. On the latter date took place the great procession to St. Giles's. First rode Sir Harry Graham, Montrose's half-brother, carrying the arms of his house. Then followed the Graham kinsmen with their different standards —Duntroon, Morphie, Cairnie, Monzie, Balgowan, Drums, Gorthie; and Black Pate of Inchbrakie, who had been with

Montrose on the August afternoon in Atholl when the curtain rose upon his campaign, bore his insignia of the Garter. The body was carried by fourteen earls, including the men, or the sons of the men, who had betrayed him—such as Seaforth, and Home, and Roxburgh, as well as old opponents like Eglinton and Callander. Twelve viscounts and barons bore the pall, among them Strathnaver, the son of the Sutherland who had locked the gates of the north after Carbisdale. The young Montrose and his brother, Lord Robert, followed the coffin, and in the procession were representatives of almost every Scottish house. Argyll's friend and Montrose's brother-in-law, Rollo, was there, and Marischal, who had held Dunnottar against him, and Tweeddale, who had voted for his death. There, too, were the faithful friends who had not failed him—Maderty and Frendraught and the Marquis of Douglas, and old Napier's grandson. The morning had been stormy, but as the procession moved from Holyrood the sun shone out brightly, as it had done at his end. The streets were lined with the trainbands, who fired their volleys, while the cannon thundered in reply from the castle, wherein lay Argyll under sentence of death. The nobles of Scotland, according to their wont, had moved over to the winning side. The pageant was an act of tardy justice, and it pleases by its dramatic contrasts, but it had small relevance to Montrose's true achievement. He was as little kin to the rabble of the Restoration as to the rabble of the Covenant. The noble monument which now marks his grave in the ancient High Kirk of Scotland is a more fitting testimony, for it has been left to modern days to recognize the greatness of one who had no place in his generation.

John Buchan, MONTROSE

*   *   *

The restoration of 1660 and Charles's accession to the thrones of Scotland and England (both had separate parliaments) established an uneasy peace. The refined differences between Catholic and Protestant theology were at once too remote and immediate for ordinary folk, and they welcomed the Revolution of 1688 which established a modest certainty—the Protestant succession. More evident in these times with the return of Charles II from France was a new sense of fun—an escape into gaiety—sometimes bawdy and reprehensible. It appeared in England before Scotland. Indeed, before it happened in Scotland the Queen in England sought to unite the two countries.

Early in 1706, the Queen appointed thirty-one Commissioners from each country. The English representation was virtually all Whig, but the Scots deliberately included some of the critics of Union including Lockhart of Carnwath, a professed Jacobite, but overlooking Hamilton; Argyll declined to act.

The Commissioners met in Whitehall on 16 April and, by 16 July, had agreed on the terms of a treaty which were to be kept secret until they were presented, first to the Scottish Parliament, and then to the English. That they achieved in nine weeks so momentous a result was due to the fact that the wise men on both sides dreaded the consequences of failure and that there were the elements of a bargain. England, at war with France, could not afford to have behind her back a hostile Scotland under a Jacobite ruler, and demanded a complete union and acceptance of the Hanoverian succession. The Scots wanted free trade at home and abroad. They would have preferred federation to complete union, but could not insist upon it since the English were adamant, and they themselves knew that the breakdown of the treaty might involve them in civil war and French intervention on behalf of a 'Popish King'.

The essential points of the Treaty were these. The two kingdoms were to be united into one in the name of Great Britain with a common flag, a common great seal and a common coinage. The monarchy of Great Britain was to descend to the Hanoverian Princess and her heirs. The two countries were to have one and the same Parliament, styled the Parliament of Great Britain; the Scottish representation in this was reckoned according to the ratio, not of populations (perhaps five to one), but of taxable capacity (about thirty-six to one) and Scotland was to send only sixteen peers to join the 190 English peers and forty-five commoners to join the 513 from England and Wales.

Scotland was to retain her own law and her own judicature free from any appeal to any court sitting in Westminster Hall; the Privy Council and the existing Court of Exchequer were to remain until the Parliament of Great Britain should think fit to make other arrangements.

Arrangements were made for an equitable distribution of public burdens with some concessions as to customs in the interest of Scotland; and, in as much as these would include the service for the National Debt (that of England was nearly £18,000,000 and that of Scotland, £160,000), Scotland was to receive a cash payment of £398,085, 10s. with a promise of a further payment at the end of seven years to balance the increased revenue to be expected from the Scottish customs and excise. The yields of these 'Equivalents' were to be used to recompense private losses due to the standardization of the coinage; to reimburse investors in the Darien Company, which was to be extinguished; to pay the public debts of the Scottish Crown and to provide, for seven years, £2,000 a year to aid wool-manufacture, fisheries, and other industries; the Scottish nobles were to keep their heritable jurisdictions, and the Scottish burghs their old privilege.

When the draft Treaty was presented to the Scottish Parliament in October 1706, and its terms became public, it was met with a howl of execration throughout the land which was, no doubt, fomented by Jacobites, but which also represented a feeling that Scotland had been sold to the English. In Edinburgh,

Glasgow, and Dumfries, there was mob violence and, as the debates in Parliament continued, petitions came in from about a third of the shires, a quarter of the royal burghs, and from some presbyteries and parishes who feared that the Kirk was in danger. None the less, when it came to the point, the Articles were approved one by one and, on 16 January 1707, the entire treaty was passed by 110 votes to sixty-nine, there being a majority in each Estate, that of the nobles being the most pronounced.

J. D. Mackie, HISTORY OF SCOTLAND

Burns a little later expressed his view of the matter:

Such a Parcel of Rogues in a Nation

Fareweel to a' our Scottish fame,
    Fareweel our ancient glory!
Fareweel ev'n to the Scottish name,
    Sae famed in martial story!
Now Sark rins over Solway sands,
    An' Tweed rins to the ocean,
To mark where England's province stands—
    Such a parcel of rogues in a nation!

What force or guile could not subdue
    Thro' many warlike ages
Is wrought now by a coward few
    For hireling traitor's wages.
The English steel we could disdain,
    Secure in valour's station;
But English gold has been our bane—
    Such a parcel of rogues in a nation!

O, would, or I had seen the day
   That Treason thus could sell us,
My auld grey head had lien in clay
   Wi' Bruce and loyal Wallace!
But pith and power, till my last hour
   I'll mak this declaration:—
'We're bought and sold for English gold'—
   Such a parcel of rogues in a nation!

Robert Burns, from THE OXFORD BOOK OF
SCOTTISH VERSE

*   *   *

Allan Ramsay is usually called the elder because of the presumably greater talents of his eldest son, the painter. But the mood may be changing, for he seems to me to introduce a new tone and stanza to Scots poetry that was to be repeated later. He is a Restoration poet in his mockery and easy bawdry, as in his handling of the last words of a famous Edinburgh bawd, Lucky Spence. The year is 1718, and to give a gloss of the Scots words would impoverish the reader's imagination.

Lucky Spence's Last Advice

Three times the carline grain'd and rifted,
Then frae the cod her pow she lifted,
In bawdy policy well gifted,
        When she now faun,
That Death na langer wad be shifted,
        She thus began:

My loving lasses, I maun leave ye,
But dinna wi' ye'r greeting grieve me,
Nor wi' your draunts and droning deave me,
                    But bring's a gill;
For faith, my bairns, ye may believe me,
                    'Tis 'gainst my will.

O black-ey'd Bess and mim-mou'd Meg,
O'er good to work or yet to beg;
Lay sunkots up for a sair leg,
                    For whan ye fail,
Ye'r face will not be worth a feg,
                    Nor yet ye'r tail.

When e'er ye meet a fool that's fow,
That ye're a maiden gar him trow,
Seem nice, but stick to him like glew;
                    And whan set down,
Drive at the jango till he spew,
                    Syne he'll sleep soun.

Whan he's asleep, then dive and catch
His ready cash, his rings or watch;
And gin he likes to light his match
                    At your spunk-box,
Ne'er stand to let the fumbling wretch
                    E'en take the pox.

Cleek a' ye can be hook or crook,
Ryp ilky poutch frae nook to nook;
Be sure to truff his pocket-book,
                    Saxty pounds Scots
Is nae deaf nits: In little bouk
                    Lie great bank-notes.

To get a mends of whinging fools,
That's frighted for repenting-stools.
Wha often, whan their metal cools,
                    Turn sweer to pay,
Gar the kirk-boxie hale the dools
                    Anither day.

But dawt Red Coats, and let them scoup,
Free for the fou of cutty stoup;
To gee them up, ye need na hope
                    E'er to do well:
They'll rive ye'r brats and kick your doup,
                    And play the Deel.

There's ae sair cross attends the craft,
That curst Correction-house, where aft
Vild Hangy's taz ye'r riggings saft
                    Makes black and blae,
Enough to pit a body daft;
                    But what'll ye say.

Nane gathers gear withouten care,
Ilk pleasure has of pain a skare;
Suppose then they should tirl ye bare,
                    And gar ye fike,
E'en learn to thole; 'tis very fair
                    Ye're nibour like.

Forby, my looves, count upo' losses,
Ye'r milk-white teeth and cheeks like roses,
Whan jet-black hair and brigs of noses,
                    Faw down wi' dads
To keep your hearts up 'neath sic crosses,
                    Set up for bawds.

Wi' well-crish'd loofs I hae been canty,
Whan e'er the lads wad fain ha'e faun t'ye;
To try the auld game Taunty Raunty,
                    Like coofers keen,
They took advice of me your aunty,
                    If ye were clean.

Then up I took my siller ca'
And whistl'd benn whiles ane, whiles twa;
Roun'd in his lug, that there was a
                    Poor country Kate,
As halesom as the well of Spaw,
                    But unka blate.

Sae whan e'er company came in,
And were upo' a merry pin,
I slade away wi' little din
                    And muckle mense,
Left conscience judge, it was a' ane
                    To Lucky Spence.

My bennison come on good doers,
Who spend their cash on bawds and whores;
May they ne'er want the wale of cures
                    For a sair snout:
Foul fa' the quacks wha that fire smoors,
                    And puts nae out.

My malison light ilka day
On them that drink, and dinna pay,
But tak a snack and rin away;
                    May't be their hap
Never to want a gonorrhœa,
                    Or rotten clap.

Lass gi'e us in anither gill,
A mutchken, Jo, let's tak our fill;
Let Death syne registrate his bill
                    Whan I want sense,
I'll slip away with better will,
                    Quo' Lucky Spence.

Allan Ramsay, from THE POEMS OF ALLAN RAMSAY
AND ROBERT FERGUSON

*   *   *

*The religious wars were over, but there were still those, mainly
Catholics, who supported the Stuart line, and in 1715 and 1745
gave expression to their loyalty. The incursions were dangerous
but they failed for two reasons: they lacked popular support, and
a general of Montrose's genius.*

Culloden and After

You understand it? How they returned from Culloden
over the soggy moors aslant, each cap
at the low ebb no new full tide could pardon:
how they stood silent at the end of the rope
unwound from battle: and to the envelope
of a bedded room came home, polite and sudden.

And how, much later, bards from Tiree and Mull
would write of exile in the hard town
where mills belched English, anger of new school:
how they remembered where the sad and brown
landscapes were dear and distant as the crown
that fuddled Charles might study in his ale.

There was a sleep. Long fences leaned across
the vacant croft. The silly cows were heard
mooing their sorrow and their Gaelic loss.
The pleasing thrush would branch upon a sword.
A mind withdrew against its dreamed hoard
as whelks withdraw or crabs their delicate claws.

And nothing to be heard but songs indeed
while wandering Charles would on his olives feed
and from his Minch of sherries mumble laws.

Iain Crichton Smith, from THE OXFORD BOOK OF
SCOTTISH VERSE

A note from the Scottish Office:

From about 1750 onward, it was mainly the turn of industry to
profit from the new creative spirit abroad in Scotland. Ironworks
and factories were built, new coalmines sunk and new shipyards
opened. Scotland's "merchant navy", for instance, grew from an
estimated 100 ships in 1700 to more than 2,000 in 1800. In 1779,
the country's first cotton mill was opened, yet by the end of the
century cotton spinning had become one of the country's leading
industries.

Economic change was accompanied by changes in the social
structure. The population itself increased from an estimated
1,100,000 at the time of the Treaty of Union to more than
1,600,000 by 1800. Art, literature, publishing and architecture
flourished. Glasgow and Edinburgh, each with a population of
around 80,000, became two of the most attractive cities in the
United Kingdom, distinguished by elegant squares, streets and
terraces, by stately civic buildings and extensive parks. Clubs,
debating societies and coffee houses contributed to the new

"sophistication", and it was not long before Edinburgh was dubbed "the Athens of the North".

SCOTLAND TODAY

Dr William Hunter of the Hunterian Museum

If the seventeenth century lay with England, in the figures of Bacon, Locke and Newton, the eighteenth century lay with Scotland with Hume and Adam Smith, the dominant figures of the Scottish Enlightenment. Hume had startled European thinkers with his Treatise of Human Nature *(1739), perhaps the first clear statement of empirical thought—you cannot derive an 'ought' from an 'is'. As Burns put it, 'facts are chiels that winna ding!' But there are some things in* An Enquiry Concerning Human Understanding *(1748) which may induce thought in a twentieth-century Scotsman.*

Our most holy religion is founded on *Faith*, not on reason; and it is a sure method of exposing it to put it to such a trial as it is, by no means, fitted to endure. To make this more evident, let us examine those miracles, related in scripture; and not to lose ourselves in too wide a field, let us confine ourselves to such as we find in the *Pentateuch*, which we shall examine, according to the principles of these pretended Christians, not as the word or testimony of God himself, but as the production of a mere human writer and historian. Here then we are first to consider a book, presented to us by a barbarous and ignorant people, written in an age when they were still more barbarous, and in all probability long after the facts which it relates, corroborated by no concurring testimony, and resembling those fabulous accounts, which every nation gives of its origin. Upon reading this book, we find it full of prodigies and miracles. It gives an account of a state of the world and of human nature entirely different from the present: Of our fall from that state: Of the age of man, extended to near a thousand years: Of the destruction of the world by a deluge: Of the arbitrary choice of one people, as the favourites of heaven; and that people the countrymen of the author: Of their deliverance from bondage by prodigies the most astonishing imaginable: I desire any one to lay his hand upon his heart, and after a serious consideration declare, whether he thinks that the falsehood of such a book,

57

supported by such a testimony, would be more extraordinary and miraculous than all the miracles it relates; which is, however, necessary to make it be received, according to the measures of probability above established.

What we have said of miracles may be applied, without any variation, to prophecies; and indeed, all prophecies are real miracles, and as such only, can be admitted as proofs of any revelation. If it did not exceed the capacity of human nature to foretell future events, it would be absurd to employ any prophecy as an argument for a divine mission or authority from heaven. So that, upon the whole, we may conclude, that the *Christian Religion* not only was at first attended with miracles, but even at this day cannot be believed by any reasonable person without one. Mere reason is insufficient to convince us of its veracity: And whoever is moved by *Faith* to assent to it, is conscious of a continued miracle in his own person, which subverts all the principles of his understanding, and gives him a determination to believe what is most contrary to custom and experience.

And on the nature of existence:

The existence [, therefore,] of any being can only be proved by arguments from its cause or its effect; and these arguments are founded entirely on experience. If we reason *a priori*, anything may appear able to produce anything. The falling of a pebble may, for aught we know, extinguish the sun; or the wish of a man control the planets in their orbits. It is only experience, which teaches us the nature and bounds of cause and effect, and enables us to infer the existence of one object from that of another. Such is the foundation of moral reasoning, which forms the greater part of human knowledge, and is the source of all human action and behaviour.

Moral reasonings are either concerning particular or general facts. All deliberations in life regard the former; as also all disquisitions in history, chronology, geography, and astronomy.

The sciences, which treat of general facts, are politics, natural philosophy, physic, chemistry, &c. where the qualities, causes and effects of a whole species of objects are enquired into.

Divinity or Theology, as it proves the existence of a Deity, and the immortality of souls, is composed partly of reasonings concerning particular, partly concerning general facts. It has a foundation in *reason*, so far as it is supported by experience. But its best and most solid foundation is *faith* and divine revelation.

Morals and criticism are not so properly objects of the understanding as of taste and sentiment. Beauty, whether moral or natural, is felt, more properly than perceived. Or if we reason concerning it, and endeavour to fix its standard, we regard a new fact, to wit, the general taste of mankind, or some such fact, which may be the object of reasoning and enquiry.

When we run over libraries, persuaded of these principles, what havoc must we make? If we take in our hand any volume; of divinity or school metaphysics, for instance; let us ask, *Does it contain any abstract reasoning concerning quantity or number?* No. *Does it contain any experimental reasoning concerning matter of fact and existence?* No. Commit it then to the flames: for it can contain nothing but sophistry and illusion.

David Hume, AN ENQUIRY CONCERNING HUMAN
UNDERSTANDING

*　　*　　*

In March 1776 Gibbon received a letter from Hume on the initial volume of the Decline and Fall, and he added a note:

A letter from Mr. Hume overpaid the labour of ten years; but I have never presumed to accept a place in the triumvirate of British historians.

That curious and original letter will amuse the reader, and his gratitude should shield my free communication from the reproach of vanity.

'Edinburgh, March 18, 1776.

'DEAR SIR,

'As I ran through your volume of history with great avidity and impatience, I cannot forbear discovering somewhat of the same impatience in returning you thanks for your agreeable present, and expressing the satisfaction which the performance has given me. Whether I consider the dignity of your style, the depth of your matter, or the extensiveness of your learning, I must regard the work as equally the object of esteem; and I own that if I had not previously had the happiness of your personal acquaintance, such a performance from an Englishman in our age would have given me some surprise. You may smile at this sentiment, but as it seems to me that your countrymen, for almost a whole generation, have given themselves up to barbarous and absurd faction, and have totally neglected all polite letters, I no longer expected any valuable production ever to come from them. I know it will give you pleasure (as it did me) to find that all the men of letters in this place concur in their admiration of your work, and in their anxious desire of your continuing it.

'When I heard of your undertaking (which was some time ago), I own I was a little curious to see how you would extricate yourself from the subject of your last two chapters. I think you have observed a very prudent temperament; but it was impossible to treat the subject so as not to give grounds of suspicion against you, and you may expect that a clamour will arise. This, if anything, will retard your success with the public: for in every other respect your work is calculated to be popular. But among many other marks of decline, the prevalence of superstition in England prognosticates the fall of philosophy and decay of taste; and though nobody be more capable than you to revive them, you will probably find a struggle in your first advances.

'I see you entertain a great doubt with regard to the authenticity of the poems of Ossian. You are certainly right in so doing. It is indeed strange that any men of sense could have imagined it possible, that above twenty thousand verses, along with numberless historical facts, could have been preserved by oral tradition during fifty generations, by the rudest, perhaps, of all the European nations, the most necessitous, the most turbulent, and the most unsettled. Where a supposition is so contrary to common sense, any positive evidence of it ought never to be regarded. Men run with great avidity to give their evidence in favour of what flatters their passions and their national prejudices. You are therefore over and above indulgent to us in speaking of the matter with hesitation.

'I must inform you that we are all very anxious to hear that you have fully collected the materials for your second volume, and that you are even considerably advanced in the composition of it. I speak this more in the name of my friends than in my own, as I cannot expect to live so long as to see the publication of it. Your ensuing volume will be more delicate than the preceding, but I trust in your prudence for extricating you from the difficulties; and, in all events, you have courage to despise the clamour of bigots.

> I am, with great regard,
> Dear Sir,
> Your most obedient, and most humble Servant,

> DAVID HUME.'

Some weeks afterwards I had the melancholy pleasure of seeing Mr. Hume in his passage through London; his body feeble, his mind firm. On the 25th of August of the same year (1776) he died, at Edinburgh, the death of a philosopher.

> David Hume to Edward Gibbon, as reflected in
> AUTOBIOGRAPHY OF EDWARD GIBBON

But the death was not to go unnoticed, nor the beliefs unchallenged. The great gadfly of the 18th century was there full of wonder—and curiosity.

AN ACCOUNT OF MY LAST INTERVIEW
WITH DAVID HUME, ESQ.

[Partly recorded in my Journal, partly enlarged from my memory, 3 March 1777.]

ON SUNDAY FORENOON the 7 of July 1776, being too late for church, I went to see Mr. David Hume, who was returned from London and Bath, just a-dying. I found him alone, in a reclining posture in his drawing-room. He was lean, ghastly, and quite of an earthy appearance. He was dressed in a suit of grey cloth with white metal buttons, and a kind of scratch wig. He was quite different from the plump figure which he used to present. He had before him Dr. Campbell's *Philosophy of Rhetoric*. He seemed to

61

be placid and even cheerful. He said he was just approaching to his end. I think these were his words. I know not how I contrived to get the subject of immortality introduced. He said he never had entertained any belief in religion since he began to read Locke and Clarke. I asked him if he was not religious when he was young. He said he was, and he used to read *The Whole Duty of Man*; that he made an abstract from the catalogue of vices at the end of it, and examined himself by this, leaving out murder and theft and such vices as he had no chance of committing, having no inclination to commit them. This, he said, was strange work; for instance, to try if, notwithstanding his excelling his schoolfellows, he had no pride or vanity. He smiled in ridicule of this as absurd and contrary to fixed principles and necessary consequences, not adverting that religious discipline does not mean to extinguish, but to moderate, the passions; and certainly an excess of pride or vanity is dangerous and generally hurtful. He then said flatly that the morality of every religion was bad, and, I really thought, was not jocular when he said that when he heard a man was religious, he concluded he was a rascal, though he had known some instances of very good men being religious. This was just an extravagant reverse of the common remark as to infidels.

I had a strong curiosity to be satisfied if he persisted in disbelieving a future state even when he had death before his eyes. I was persuaded from what he now said, and from his manner of saying it, that he did persist. I asked him if it was not possible that there might be a future state. He answered it was possible that a piece of coal put upon the fire would not burn; and he added that it was a most unreasonable fancy that we should exist for ever. That immortality, if it were at all, must be general; that a great proportion of the human race has hardly any intellectual qualities; that a great proportion dies in infancy before being possessed of reason; yet all these must be immortal; that a porter who gets drunk by ten o'clock with gin must be immortal; that the trash of every age must be preserved, and that new universes must be created to contain such infinite numbers. This appeared to me an unphilosophical objection, and I said, "Mr. Hume, you know spirit does not take up space."

I may illustrate what he last said by mentioning that in a former conversation with me on this subject he used pretty much the same mode of reasoning, and urged that Wilkes and his mob must be immortal. One night last May as I was coming up King Street, Westminster, I met Wilkes, who carried me into Parliament Street to see a curious procession pass: the funeral of a lamplighter attended by some hundreds of his fraternity with torches. Wilkes, who either is, or affects to be, an infidel, was rattling away, "I think there's an end of that fellow. I think he won't rise again." I very calmly said to him, "You bring into my mind the strongest argument that ever I heard against a future state"; and then told him David Hume's objection that Wilkes and his mob must be immortal. It seemed to make a proper impression, for he grinned abashment, as a Negro grows whiter when he blushes. But to return to my last interview with Mr. Hume.

I asked him if the thought of annihilation never gave him any uneasiness. He said not the least; no more than the thought that he had not been, as Lucretius observes. "Well," said I, "Mr. Hume, I hope to triumph over you when I meet you in a future state; and remember you are not to pretend that you was joking with all this infidelity." "No, no," said he. "But I shall have been so long there before you come that it will be nothing new." In this style of good humour and levity did I conduct the conversation. Perhaps it was wrong on so awful a subject. But as nobody was present, I thought it could have no bad effect. I however felt a degree of horror, mixed with a sort of wild, strange, hurrying recollection of my excellent mother's pious instructions, of Dr. Johnson's noble lessons, and of my religious sentiments and affections during the course of my life. I was like a man in sudden danger eagerly seeking his defensive arms; and I could not but be assailed by momentary doubts while I had actually before me a man of such strong abilities and extensive inquiry dying in the persuasion of being annihilated. But I maintained my faith. I told him that I believed the Christian religion as I believed history. Said he: "You do not believe it as you believe the Revolution." "Yes," said I; "but the difference is that I am not so much interested in the truth of the Revolution; otherwise I should have anxious doubts concerning it. A man who is in love has doubts of the affection of his mistress, without cause." I mentioned Soame Jenyns's little book in defence of Christianity, which was just published but which I had not yet read. Mr. Hume said, "I am told there is nothing of his usual spirit in it."

He had once said to me, on a forenoon while the sun was shining bright, that he did not wish to be immortal. This was a most wonderful thought. The reason he gave was that he was very well in this state of being, and that the chances were very much against his being so well in another state; and he would rather not be more than be worse. I answered that it was reasonable to hope he would be better; that there would be a progressive improvement. I tried him at this interview with that topic, saying that a future state was surely a pleasing idea. He said no, for that it was always seen through a gloomy medium; there was always a Phlegethon or a hell. "But," said I, "would it not be agreeable to have hopes of seeing our friends again?" and I mentioned three men lately deceased, for whom I knew he had a high value: Ambassador Keith, Lord Alemoor, and Baron Mure. He owned it would be agreeable, but added that none of them entertained such a notion. I believe he said, such a foolish, or such an absurd, notion; for he was indecently and impolitely positive in incredulity. "Yes," said I, "Lord Alemoor was a believer." David acknowledged that *he* had *some* belief.

I somehow or other brought Dr. Johnson's name into our conversation. I had often heard him speak of that great man in a very illiberal manner. He said upon this occasion, "Johnson should be pleased with my *History*." Nettled by Hume's frequent attacks upon my revered friend in former conversations, I told him now that Dr. Johnson did not allow him much credit; for he said, "Sir, the fellow is a Tory by chance." I am sorry that I mentioned this at such a time. I was off my guard; for the truth is that Mr. Hume's pleasantry was such that there was no solemnity in the scene; and death for the time did not seem dismal. It surprised me to find him talking of different matters with a tranquillity of mind and a clearness of head which few men possess at any time. Two particulars I remember: Smith's *Wealth of Nations*, which he commended much, and Monboddo's *Origin of Language*, which he treated contemptuously. I said, "If I were you, I should regret annihilation. Had I written such an admirable history, I should be sorry to leave it." He said, "I shall leave that history, of which you are pleased to speak so favourably, as perfect as I can." He said, too, that all the great abilities with which men had ever been endowed were relative to this world. He said he became a greater friend to the Stuart family as he advanced in studying for his history; and he hoped he had vindicated the two first of them so effectually that they would never again be attacked.

Mr. Lauder, his surgeon, came in for a little, and Mr. Mure, the Baron's son, for another small interval. He was, as far as I could judge, quite easy with both. He said he had no pain, but was wasting away. I left him with impressions which disturbed me for some time.

(ADDITIONS FROM MEMORY 22 JANUARY 1778.) Speaking of his singular notion that men of religion were generally bad men, he said, "One of the men" (or "The man"—I am not sure which) "of the greatest honour that I ever knew is my Lord Marischal, who is a downright atheist. I remember I once hinted something as if I believed in the being of God, and he would not speak to me for a week." He said this with his usual grunting pleasantry, with that thick breath which fatness had rendered habitual to him, and that smile of simplicity which his good humour constantly produced.

When he spoke against Monboddo, I told him that Monboddo said to me that he believed the abusive criticism upon his book in *The Edinburgh Magazine and Review* was written by Mr. Hume's direction. David seemed irritated, and said, "Does the *scoundrel"* (I am sure either *that* or*"rascal"*) "say so?" He then told me that he had observed to one of the Faculty of Advocates that Monboddo was wrong in his observation that

and gave as a proof of the line in Milton. When the review came out, he found this very remark in it, and said to that advocate, "Oho! I have discovered you"—reminding him of the circumstance.*

It was amazing to find him so keen in such a state. I must add one other circumstance which is material, as it shows that he perhaps was not without some hope of a future state, and that his spirits were supported by a consciousness (or at least a notion) that his conduct had been virtuous. He said, "If there were a future state, Mr. Boswell, I think I could give as good an account of my life as most people."

* Boswell never filled the blank.

James Boswell, from BOSWELL IN EXTREMES

In the year Hume died, Adam Smith's The Wealth of Nations *was published.*

The annual labour of every nation is the fund which originally supplies us with all the necessaries and conveniences of life which it annually consumes, and which consists always either in the immediate produce of that labour, or in what is purchased with that produce from other nations.

It is not from the benevolence of the butcher, the brewer, or the baker that we expect our dinner, but from their regard to their own interest. We address ourselves, not to their humanity, but to their self-love, and never talk to them of their own necessities, but of their advantages.

On the investment of capital by the capitalist
He generally, indeed, neither intends to promote the public interest, nor knows how much he is promoting it. He intends only his own gain, and he is in this, as in other cases, led by an invisible hand to promote an end which was no part of his intention.

On the objectivity of commerce
A country that has no mines of its own must undoubtedly draw its gold and silver from foreign countries in the same manner as one that has no vineyards of its own must draw its wines. It does not seem necessary, however, that the attention of the government should be more turned towards the one than the other object.

On the value and use, the Paradox of Value
The things which have the greatest value in use have frequently little or no value in exchange; and, on the contrary, those which have the greatest value in exchange have frequently little or no value in use. Nothing is more useful than water; but it will purchase scarce anything; scarce anything can be had in exchange for it. A diamond, on the contrary, has scarce any value in use; but a very great quantity of other goods may frequently be had in exchange for it.

The nature of exchange
If among a nation of hunters, for example, it usually costs twice the labour to kill a beaver which it does to kill a deer, one beaver should naturally exchange for or be worth two deer.

The motive of trade
But man has almost constant occasion for the help of his brethren, and it is vain for him to expect it from their benevolence alone. He will be more likely to prevail if he can interest their self-love in his favour, and show them that it is for their own advantage to do for him what he requires of them.

In the year of The Wealth of Nations *(1776) the American colonies declared their independence of Britain. Adam Smith exercised much influence on the development of the United States economy.*

The statesman who should attempt to direct private people in what manner they ought to employ their capitals, would not only load himself with a most unnecessary attention, but assume an authority which could safely be trusted to no council whatever, and which would nowhere be so dangerous as in the hands of a man who had the folly and presumption to fancy himself fit to exercise it. . . .

I have never known much good done by those who affected to trade for the public good.

Adam Smith, extracts from THE WEALTH OF NATIONS

*   *   *

From the Scottish Office again:

The present dispensation has come about in the time-honoured British fashion through a blend of evolution and expediency, tempered by a sense of what is just and fair. The process can in fact be traced back to the Treaty of Union which, though specific on a number of important points, did not make any reference to the machinery of central government. In the event, however, the new British Parliament created the special post of Secretary of State for Scottish Affairs. At the Westminster Parliament Scotland was represented by 45 Members in the House of Commons and by 16 elected peers in the House of Lords.

It may not have been an ideal arrangement, but it was the best Scotland could get at the time from a Government with whom the

68

idea of a Scottish Minister with a political enclave of his own was not at all popular. As a result, when Bonnie Prince Charlie landed in Scotland in 1745 to lead the last Jacobite uprising, advantage was taken of the occasion to abolish the office of Scottish Secretary in the interests of "national unity".

Thereafter, ultimate responsibility for Scottish affairs was vested in the British Home Secretary, and there it remained for 140 years. In practice during this long "interregnum", Scotland was governed by successive Cabinet Ministers, known as "the Scottish managers", who were either Scots or who pretended to some knowledge of Scottish affairs. Most famous of these was Henry Dundas, nicknamed "King Henry the Ninth", who "managed" Scotland efficiently though unimaginatively from 1775 to 1804. In time, Scotland itself became known as "North Britain"—which is comment enough on its loss of status.

SCOTLAND TODAY

It was that same Henry Dundas who recruited so many young Scots for the East India Company. Following the American Revolution, in 1789 the French Revolution directed people's thoughts towards liberty, equality and fraternity, by getting rid of the absolute monarchy. Britain had already solved the problem by evolving a controlling parliament in concord with a formal constitutional monarchy. Britain was the only major power in Europe sufficiently uninhibited to take advantage of the range of opportunities now open—the discovery of new lands, the expansion of science, the explosion of industry, Christian mission and romanticism in art.

Scotland participated in all. It was a hope of Burns.

A Man's a Man For A' That

Is there for honest poverty
   That hings his head, an' a' that?
The coward slave, we pass him by—
   We dare be poor for a' that!
For a' that, an' a' that!
   Our toils obscure, an' a' that,
The rank is but the guinea's stamp,
   The man's the gowd for a' that,

What though on hamely fare we dine,
   Wear hoddin grey an' a' that?
Gie fools their silks, and knaves their wine—
   A man's a man for a' that.
For a' that, an' a' that,
   Their tinsel show, an' a' that,
The honest man, tho' e'er sae poor,
   Is king o' men for a' that.

Ye see yon birkie ca'd 'a lord',
   Wha struts, an' stares, an' a' that?
Tho' hundreds worship at his word,
   He's but a cuif for a' that.
For a' that, an' a' that,
   His ribband, star, an' a' that,
The man o' independent mind,
   He looks an' laughs at a' that.

A prince can mak a belted knight,
   A marquis, duke, an' a' that!
But an honest man's aboon his might—
   Guid faith, he mauna fa' that.
For a' that, an' a' that,
   Their dignities, an' a' that,
The pith o' sense an' pride o' worth
   Are higher rank than a' that.

Then let us pray that come it may
   (As come it will for a' that)
That Sense and Worth o'er a' the earth
   Shall bear the gree an' a' that!
For a' that, an' a' that,
   It's comin yet for a' that,
That man to man the world o'er
   Shall brithers be for a' that.

Robert Burns, from THE OXFORD BOOK OF
SCOTTISH VERSE

*In Alloway in Ayrshire on a tempestuous night in January 1759
Burns was born, and his short life of genius was riven by
unnatural streaks of fortune that only his unique gift made
bearable.*

Here was a man who was at the same time, for reasons suited to
his various correspondents, both dying and recovering!

Jessy Lewars had been sending him the home news; but only
now, having given the salt-water treatment a fair trial, did he write
her a letter that was for Jean. 'My dearest love,' he wrote—

' . . . It would be injustice to deny that it has eased my pains, and I think has
strengthened me; but my appetite is still extremely bad. No flesh nor fish can I
swallow; porridge and milk are the only things I can taste. . . . I will see you on
Sunday.—Your affectionate husband,   R. B.'

Sunday, however, found him still at the Brow, and the following
Sunday also. For all that Dr. Maxwell might say, riding eleven
miles was out of the question, and there was some difficulty in
getting free conveyance. The weather was 'very rainy, coarse and
boisterous' and he dared not risk a wetting. A Dumfries baker's
van had failed him. At length he was promised a gig—the first
seen in Scotland—by a local famer, Clark of Lockerwoods.

During the week Syme rode out bringing Cunningham's reply which had been sent with privately anxious inquiries through Ryedale. Cunningham was doing his best with the Excise but could guarantee nothing. Syme was scared by Robin's looks. But he could still hope that 'the vigor of his former stamina will conquer his present illness.'

On the day following the letter to Jean the amazing invalid had walked inland by field paths and beside flowering hedges—a quarter of a mile each way—to drink tea with two more ladies, the wife and daughter of the minister of Ruthwell. It was actually fine, and the sun at setting poured in to the Manse windows. The younger woman, horrified by the visitor's sunlit face, which showed him like a corpse but for the glowing, still dangerous eyes, went to pull down the blind. But Robert stayed her hand with one of his warm smiles that charmed her as it had charmed so many other women. 'Thank you, my dear, for your kind attention,' he said, 'but oh! let him shine! He will not shine long for me!'

The fatigue of this visit brought on a fresh attack of fever next day, and he could not start for home till 3 o'clock on the afternoon of Monday, the 18th. When, that evening, he climbed down from the spring-cart at the bottom of the Mill Vennel which was too steep for the horse, he could not stand upright. But Jessy was there. Crouching and tottering, with a parched tongue, a rigor in all his being, and looks that were 'hollow and ghastly,' he managed with her help to reach his own door. Jean was 'quite speechless' with terror. They could not get him up to the smaller of the two upstairs rooms, where the yellow boxwood bed had been prepared for him, so he was put into the kitchen bed. At once he sank into an intermittent stupor.

But an urgent word would bring him out of it for half an hour together and he kept begging Jean to 'touch him and remind him when he was going wrong.' When Findlater or Lewars called he gave them his dying orders lightly and rationally. 'Don't let the Awkward Squad fire over me!' he begged one of his fellow Volunteers; and at night he managed to write at least one letter—a second summons to Mrs. Armour to come at once. [Mrs. Armour was away in Fife.] He was able also to read the letter—kindly enough, but guarded and disapproving—which came at last from Mrs. Dunlop.

Then for a time his follies, sins and failures came all at once to mind, and seeing how he was leaving Jean and the children he took the full blame on himself in an agony of penitence and self-accusation terrible to see. He must not die. Maxwell had pronounced him to be better. Repeatedly in delirium he called for Cunningham and for Syme, and when, first thing on Tuesday morning, Syme came in and took his hand he 'made a wonderful exertion.' 'I am much better to-day,' he said, raising his voice strongly, 'I shall soon be well again, for I command my spirits and my mind. But yesterday I resigned myself to death.' Seeing his face and Jean's, Syme went without hope. But 'never, never to despair' was still Robin's motto. Having left him for a few minutes alone Jean came back into the room to find the bed empty and himself sitting in a corner with the bed-clothes about him. He was 'building Resolve'—though not, alas, 'on Reason.' It took the two women to coax him back to bed. Knowing as they did that his strength was gone, they whispered together that he must have had some kind of a fit. The next day, Wednesday, they heard him shout very loudly and peremptorily for 'Gilbert! Gilbert!' but Gilbert was not there.

On Wednesday night he lapsed into a condition in which the doctors were compelled to see that his heart could not hold out much longer, and his brain refused to take in the good news which now, too late for his consolation, kept arriving at the house by letter or word of mouth—that James Burness gladly sent £10; that Thomson, by return, sent £5 and a practical suggestion for a subscribed edition of songs; that Fintry assured him of so slight a diminution of salary that the enclosed donation of £5 would cover it.

Jessy was his only consolation. She had put the four little boys to sleep at her house and had come herself to sleep with Jean. All that night Dr. Maxwell sat by Robert's bed and in the very early morning two neighbours took his place. Jessy, seeing for herself that the end was near, ran for the children who, in the true Scottish fashion, must assemble to see their father draw his last breath. The four, headed by ten-year-old Robert, stood round the bed. But here were to be no pious injunctions. The poet roused himself: he looked passionately at his boys: and with passion he cursed by name the attorney, Mr. Penn, who had sent in the bill for his Volunteer uniform. It is even said that in that extreme moment he made one last desperate effort, and that his nerves served him so far that he rose to his feet in the bed and stepped eagerly forward. Though 'much the child of disaster' and with all his errors on his forehead, the son of William Burnes would have no one say he had not played the man. But from that he relapsed into unconsciousness, and by five o'clock in the morning, into death.

Jessy took the children out for a walk along the river banks, and they brought back bunches of wild flowers and grasses and sprigs of birch and hazel and hawthorn to strew over the dead poet. Jessy knew the growing things he liked best. He had shown her one of the last fragmentary poems now thrust among the disordered papers in his desk—

> 'In gowany glens the burnie strays,
> Where bonnie lasses bleach their claes;
> Or trots by hazelly shaws and braes
>   Wi' hawthorns gray,
> Where blackbirds join the shepherd's lays
>   At close o' day.'

And though it was too late in the year for some of his favourite plants to be in blossom, she and the boys found daisies and foxgloves and harebells and some late dog-roses. Her brother, the gauger, came in and sat laboriously writing letters for Jean. Jean, sitting by her hard-won husband's body, could do little more than wonder when her pains would come upon her.

But she had many helpers now from near and far. As soon as the news got about in Dumfries, the house was busy with callers.

Men and women quite suddenly realised that here lay one who was the Poet of his Country—perhaps of mankind—as none had been before, because none before had combined so many human weaknesses with so great an ardour of living and so generous a warmth of admission. Certainly none had ever possessed a racier gift of expression for his own people. The more for having sinned on all points wherein the common man is tempted to sin, both to glory and repentance; the more for having walked the valley of the shadow of compromise while yet retaining in his breast the proud, soft, defiant heart of a man. Burns was perceived by many to be the jewel of Scotland, death sometimes has a way of giving these sudden insights.

Catherine Carswell, THE LIFE OF ROBERT BURNS

Mozart, Schubert, Shelley, Keats—it was an age when it was fashionable for genius to die young. Burns was 37.

Burns's hope of brotherhood was not to be practised in Scotland. The barbarities of civil war, the treachery of Glencoe, and as economics came to control policy, the clearances and the famine, wiped the land clear of community. It is a question whether the beauty of these eyeless spaces compensated for the loss of civilisation.

For the Old Highlands

That old lonely lovely way of living
in Highland places—twenty years a-growing,
twenty years flowering, twenty years declining—
father to son, mother to daughter giving
ripe tradition; peaceful bounty flowing;
one harmony all tones of life combining—
old, wise ways, passed like the dust blowing.

That harmony of folk and land is shattered,—
the yearly rhythm of things, the social graces,
peat-fire and music, candle-light and kindness.
Now they are gone it seems they never mattered,
much, to the world, those proud and violent races,
clansmen and chiefs whose passioned greed and blindness
made desolate these lovely lonely places.

Douglas Young, from MODERN SCOTTISH POETRY

Rousseau in Switzerland, Fielding in England, Goethe in Germany, Stendhal in France, Scott in Scotland—the romantic novel had descended on Europe. Scott's achievement in literature is so enormous it must saturate and obliterate all other activity.

A poem, and a tribute by Buchan:

Proud Maisie

Proud Maisie is in the wood,
    Walking so early;
Sweet Robin sits on the bush,
    Singing so rarely.

"Tell me, thou bonny bird,
    When shall I marry me?"
"When six braw gentlemen
    Kirkward shall carry ye."

"Who makes the bridal bed,
    Birdie, say truly?"
"The grey-headed sexton
    That delves the grave duly.

The glow-worm o'er grave and stone
    Shall light thee steady.
The owl from the steeple sing,
    Welcome, proud lady."

Sir Walter Scott, from THE OXFORD BOOK OF SCOTTISH
VERSE

Scott had not the metaphysical turn of his countrymen, and he had no instinct to preach, but the whole of his life and work was based on a reasoned philosophy of conduct. Its corner-stones were humility and discipline. The life of man was difficult, but not desperate, and to live it worthily you must forget yourself and love others. The failures were the egotists who were wrapped up in self, the doctrinaires who were in chains to a dogma, the Pharisees who despised their brethren. In him the "common sense" of the eighteenth century was coloured and lit by Christian charity. Happiness could only be attained by the unselfregarding. He preaches this faith through the mouth of Jeanie Deans—indeed it is the basis of all his ethical portraiture, it crops up everywhere in his letters and *Journal*, and in his review of Canto III of *Childe Harold* in the *Quarterly* he expounds it to Byron and labours to reconcile him with the world. This paper should not be forgotten, for in it Scott professes explicitly his moral code. Its axiom is that there is no royal road to heart's ease, but that there is a path for the humble pilgrim. The precepts for such are—

to narrow our wishes and desires within the scope of our present powers of attainment; to consider our misfortunes as our inevitable share in the patrimony of Adam; to bridle those irritable feelings which, ungoverned, are sure to become governors; to shun that intensity of galling and self-wounding reflection which our poet has described in his own burning language; to stoop, in short, to the realities of life, repent if we have offended, and pardon if we have been trespassed against; to look on the world less as our foe than as a doubtful and capricious friend whose applause we ought as far as possible to deserve, but neither to court nor to condemn.

To this philosophy he added a stalwart trust in the Christian doctrines, a trust which was simple, unqualified and unquestioning. His was not a soul to be troubled by doubts or to be kindled to mystical fervour, though he was ready to admit the reality of the latter. There is a passage in the *Journal* where he defends the work of Methodism as "carrying religion into classes in society where it would scarce be found to penetrate, did it rely merely upon proof of its doctrines, upon calm reasoning, and upon rational argument." But such excitements were not for him; for his mind to seek them would have been like drug-taking, a renunciation of self-discipline. In the Scotland of his day this teaching was much in season. The old fires of Calvinism had burned too murkily, the light of the *Aufklärung* had been too thin and cold, but in Scott was a spirit which could both illumine and comfort his world. He gave it a code of ethics robuster because more rational, and he pointed the road to a humaner faith.

John Buchan, SIR WALTER SCOTT

George Gordon Byron was born in London in 1788; the following year his mother, Lady Jean Gordon took him to Aberdeen, where they had lodgings in Queen Street. On 2 August 1791 his father died in France, and Lady Jean moved to a flat at 64 Broad Street, Aberdeen. During the years 1794 to 1798 Byron attended the Aberdeen Grammar School. On 21 May 1798 the Fifth Lord Byron died, and George Gordon Byron became the Sixth Baron Byron of Rochdale. In August of the same year he accompanied his mother to Newstead Abbey, the ancestral estate. Early in the new century he wrote a letter giving among other things the first intimation of a famous swim.

Salsette frigate. May 3d. 1810
in the Dardanelles off Abydos

My dear Drury,—When I left England nearly a year ago you
requested me to write to you.—I will do so.—I have crossed
Portugal, traversed the South of Spain, visited Sardinia, Sicily,
Malta, and thence passed into Turkey where I am still
wandering.—I first landed in Albania the ancient Epirus where
we penetrated as far as Mount Tomerit, excellently treated by the
Chief Ali Pacha, and after journeying through Illyria, Chaonia,
&ctr, crossed the Gulph of Actium with a guard of 50 Albanians
and passed the Achelous in our route through Acarnania and
Ætolia.—We stopped a short time in the Morea, crossed the
gulph of Lepanto and landed at the foot of Parnassus, saw all that
Delphi retains and so on to Thebes and Athens at which last we
remained ten weeks.—His majesty's ship Pylades brought us to
Smyrna but not before we had topographised Attica including of
course Marathon, and the Sunian Promontory.—From Smyrna
to the Troad which we visited when at anchor for a fortnight off
the Tomb of Antilochus, was our next stage, and now we are in
the Dardanelles waiting for a wind to proceed to
Constantinople.—This morning I *swam* from *Sestos* to *Abydos*,
the immediate distance is not above a mile but the current renders
it hazardous, so much so, that I doubt whether Leander's
conjugal powers must not have been exhausted in his passage to
Paradise.—I attempted it a week ago and failed owing to the
North wind and the wonderful rapidity of the tide, though I have
been from my childhood a strong swimmer, but this morning
being calmer I succeeded and crossed the "broad Hellespont" in
an hour and ten minutes.——Well, my dear Sir, I have left my
home and seen part of Africa & Asia and a tolerable portion of
Europe.—I have been with Generals, and Admirals, Princes and
Pachas, Governors and Ungovernables, but I have not time or
paper to expatiate. I wish to let you know that I live with a friendly
remembrance of you and a hope to meet you again, and if I do
this as shortly as possible, attribute it to any-thing but

forgetfulness.—Greece ancient and modern you know too well to require description. Albania indeed I have seen more of than any Englishman (but a Mr. Leake) for it is a country rarely visited from the savage character of the natives, though abounding in more natural beauties than the classical regions of Greece, which however are still eminently beautiful, particularly Delphi, and Cape Colonna in Attica.—Yet these are nothing to parts of Illyria, and Epirus, where places without a name, and rivers not laid down in maps, may one day when more known be justly esteemed superior subjects for the pencil, and the pen, than the dry ditch of the Ilissus, and the bogs of Bœotia.—The Troad is a fine field for conjecture and Snipe-shooting, and a good sportsman and an ingenious scholar may exercise their feet and faculties to great advantage upon the spot, or if they prefer riding lose their way (as I did) in a cursed quagmire of the Scamander who wriggles about as if the Dardan virgins still offered their wonted tribute. The only vestige of Troy, or her destroyers, are the barrows supposed to contain the carcases of Achilles[,] Antilochus, Ajax &c. but Mt. Ida is still in high feather, though the Shepherds are nowadays not much like Ganymede.—But why should I say more of these things? are they not written in the *Boke* of Gell? and has not Hobby got a journal? I keep none as I have renounced scribbling.—I see not much difference between ourselves & the Turks, save that we have foreskins and they none, that they have long dresses and we short, and that we talk much and they little.—In England the vices in fashion are whoring & drinking, in Turkey, Sodomy & smoking, we prefer a girl and a bottle, they a pipe and pathic.—They are sensible people, Ali Pacha told me he was sure I was a man of rank because I had *small ears* and hands and *curling hair*.—By the bye, I speak the Romaic or Modern Greek tolerably, it does not differ from the ancient dialects so much as you would conceive, but the pronunciation is diametrically opposite, of verse except in rhyme they have no idea.—I like the Greeks, who are plausible rascals, with all the Turkish vices without their courage.—However some are brave and all are beautiful, very much resembling the busts of Alcibiades, the women not quite so handsome.—I can swear in Turkish, but except one horrible oath, and "*pimp*" and "bread" and "water" I have got no great vocabulary in that language.—They are extremely polite to strangers of any rank properly protected, and as I have got 2 servants and two soldiers we get on with great eclât. We have been occasionally in danger of thieves & once of shipwreck but always escaped.—At Malta I fell in love with a married woman and challenged an aid du camp of Genl. Oakes (a rude fellow who grinned at something, I never rightly knew what,) but he explained and apologised, and the lady embarked for Cadiz, & so I escaped murder and adultery.—Of Spain I sent some account to our Hodgson, but I have subsequently written to no one save notes to relations and lawyers to keep them out of my premises.—I mean to give up all connection on my return with many of my best friends as I supposed them, and to snarl all my life, but I hope to have one good humoured laugh with you, and to embrace Dwyer and pledge Hodgson, before I commence Cynicism.—Tell Dr. Butler I am now writing with the gold pen he gave me before I left England, which is the reason my scrawl is more unentelligible [*sic*] than usual.—I have been at Athens and seen plenty of those reeds for scribbling, some of which he refused to bestow upon me because topographer Gell had brought them from Attica.— —But I will not describe, no, you must be satisfied with simple detail till my return, and then we will unfold the floodgates of Colloquoy.—I am in a 36 gun frigate going up to fetch Bob Adair from Constantinople, who will have the honour to carry this letter.—And so Hobby's *boke* is out, with some sentimental singsong of mine own to fill up, and how does it take? eh! and where the devil is the 2d Edition of my Satire with additions? and my name on the title page? and more lines tagged to the end with a new exordium and what not, hot from my anvil before I cleared the Channel?—The Mediterranean and the Atlantic roll between me and Criticism, and the thunders of the Hyberborean Review are deafened by the roar of the Hellespont.—Remember me to Claridge if not translated to College, and present to Hodgson assurances of my high consideration.—Now, you will ask, what shall I do next? and I answer I do not know, I may return in a few months, but I have intents and projects after visiting Constantinople, Hobhouse however will probably be back in September.—On the 2d. of July we have left Albion one year, "oblitus meorum, obliviscendus et illis," I was sick of my own country, and not much pre-possessed in favour of any other, but I drag on "my chain" without "lengthening it at each remove".—I am like the jolly miller caring for nobody and not cared for. All countries are much the same in my eyes, I smoke and stare at mountains, and twirl my mustachios very independently, I miss no comforts, and the Musquïtoes that rack the morbid frame of Hobhouse, have luckily for me little effect on mine because I live more temperately.—I omitted Ephesus in my Catalogue, which I visited during my sojourn at Smyrna,—but the temple has almost perished, and St. Paul need not trouble himself to epistolize the present brood of Ephesians who have converted a large church built entirely of marble into a Mosque, and I dont know that the edifice looks the worse for it.—My paper is full and my ink ebbing, Good Afternoon!—If you address to me at Malta, the letter will be forwarded wherever I may be.—Hobhouse greets you, he pines for his poetry, at least some tidings of it.—I almost forgot to tell you that I am dying for love of three Greek Girls at Athens, sisters, two of whom have promised to accompany me to England, I lived in the same house, Teresa, Mariana, and Kattinka, are the names of these divinities all of them under 15.—your ταπεινοτατοσ δουλοσ [your humble servant]

BYRON

from BYRON'S LETTERS AND JOURNALS

*   *   *

82

The Indian Recurrence
On the last day of the sixteenth century Queen Elizabeth gave the East India Company its charter: "Know ye therefore . . . that they shall be a body Corporate and Public in deed and in name by the name of the Governor and Company of merchants of London trading into the East Indies." One of the benefits of the Act of Union was to bring young Scots more actively into the Company's business. Of the four great figures who guided the sub-continent into the nineteenth century and shaped its destiny, three were Scots—Munro, Elphinstone and Boy Malcolm.

Boy Malcolm

Malcolm was older in service than Elphinstone by some ten years. He was a grandson of the manse, his father being a small farmer in Eskdale. He was one of seventeen children and when his father fell suddenly into financial trouble it became necessary to settle as many sons as possible. The Directors of the East India Company were doubtful whether they could stretch things so far as to commission a boy of thirteen. "Why, my little man," said one of them playfully, "what would you do if you met Hyder Ali?" (he being the father of Tippoo and the ogre of the moment). "I would draw my sword and cut off his heid," replied the candidate, and was commissioned at once with acclamation.

Munro

"Whenever we are obliged to resign our sovreignty we should leave the natives so far improved from their connection with us, as to be capable of maintaining a free, or at least regular, government among themselves."

Elphinstone

"The most desirable death for us to die should be the improvement of the natives reaching such a pitch as would render it impossible for a foreign nation to retain the government . . ."

Philip Woodruff, as reported in THE MEN WHO RULED INDIA

At home and after Culloden, the clan still flourished.

The science of Armory, or Heraldry, as a system of identification, was evolved in the twelfth century. Leaders adopted simple and outstanding devices which they painted on their shields and banners, so that their followers might recognise them in war, and the same device was repeated on the shirt worn over the armour, hence the term 'coat of arms.' In Scotland the *leine croich*, or saffron shirt of war, was in some cases evidently the basis upon which heraldic objects were depicted, but in other cases a small shield was embroidered on the back and breast of the yellow *leine croich*. Armorial bearings, when invented, were a personal mark of identification, but necessarily became hereditary in the second generation (end of twelfth century), when the son who succeeded to estate or Chiefship naturally continued the banner, shield, and surcoat which his father's followers had learnt to recognise, and since a coat of arms could only distinguish one individual, his younger brothers were obliged to bear marks of cadency to distinguish them from the head of the house. In peace the banner above a house, or arms carved upon it, indicated the owner, and a wax seal displaying a representation of the owner's shield was attached to charters, and served as a signature, which could be recognised by those who could not read.

Arms, from their nature and the position of those who first used them, became marks of *nobility*, and as grants of nobility included a grant of arms, a grant of arms became legally a patent of nobility and proof of inheritance of arms a proof of nobility.

Sir Thomas Innes of Learney, THE TARTANS OF THE CLANS AND FAMILIES OF SCOTLAND

*   *   *

Great Seal of King David II, showing armorial shield, tabard (surcoat), and horse-trappings (ordinary lairds carried their own banners, but the King's banner—also showing the tressured lion rampant—is carried by the Chief of the Scrymgeours). This illustration shows just how arms were used. (No crest is depicted—they were often omitted in battle.)

The eighteenth century had not been one of great movement for Scotsmen outside the land. Hume was royally entertained when he went abroad but in spite of the appalling physical conditions of the land, the Scottish Enlightenment crystallized round the universities, and the two great writers of the century, Scott and Burns, spent most of their time at home. Scott existed into the nineteenth century. Now Hogg, perhaps with an ironic nod towards Ossian and a more considered judgement of Provence in the Middle Ages, and aware that the Scottish practice towards witchcraft in the earlier centuries had been most unenlightened and vicious, turned his great talents to that borderland where imagination and reality live in distrust and wonder.

> There was a king, and a courteous king,
>   And he had a daughter sae bonnie;
> And he lo'ed that maiden aboon a' thing
>   I' the bonnie, bonnie halls o' Binnorie.
>
> But wae be to thee, thou warlock wight,
>   My malison come o'er thee,
> For thou hast undone the bravest knight,
>   That ever brak bread i' Binnorie!
>
> *Old Song*

The days of the Stuarts, kings of Scotland, were the days of chivalry and romance. The long and bloody contest that the nation maintained against the whole power of England, for the recovery of its independence,—of those rights which had been most unwarrantably wrested from our fathers by the greatest and most treacherous sovereign of that age, with the successful and glorious issue of the war, laid the foundation for this spirit of heroism, which appears to have been at its zenith about the time that the Stuarts first acquired the sovereignty of the realm. The deeds of the Douglasses, the Randolphs, and other border barons of that day, are not to be equalled by any recorded in our annals; while the reprisals that they made upon the English, in retaliation for former injuries, enriched both them and their followers, and rendered their appearance splendid and imposing to a degree that would scarcely now gain credit. It was no uncommon thing for a Scottish earl then to visit the Court at the head of a thousand horsemen, all splendidly mounted in their military accoutrements; and many of these gentlemen of rank and family. In court and camp, feats of arms were the topic of conversation, and the only die that stamped the character of a man of renown, either with the fair, the monarch, or the chiefs of the land. No gentleman of noble blood would pay his addresses to his mistress, until he had broken a spear with the knights of the rival nation, surprised a stronghold, or driven a prey from the kinsmen of the Piercies, the Musgraves, or the Howards. As in all other things that run to a fashionable extremity, the fair sex took the lead in encouraging these deeds of chivalry, till it came to have the appearance of a national mania. There were tournaments at the castle of every feudal baron and knight. The ploughman and drivers were often discovered, on returning from the fields, hotly engaged in a tilting bout with their goads and plough-staves; and even the little boys and maidens on the village green, each well mounted on a crooked stick, were daily engaged in the combat, and riding rank and file against each other, breaking their tiny weapons in the furious onset, while the mimic fire flashed from their eyes. Then was the play of *Scots and English* begun, a favourite one on the school green to this day. Such was the spirit of the age, not only in Scotland, but over all the countries of southern Europe, when the romantic incidents occurred on which the following tale is founded. It was taken down from the manuscript of an old Curate, who had spent the latter part of his life in the village of Mireton, and was given to the present Editor by one of those tenants who now till the valley where stood the richest city of this realm.

There were once a noble king and queen of Scotland, as many in that land have been.—In this notable tell-tale manner, does old Isaac, the curate, begin his narrative. It will be seen in the sequel, that this king and queen were Robert the Second and his consort.—They were beloved by all their subjects, (continues he,) and loved and favoured them in return; and the country enjoyed happiness and peace, all save a part adjoining to the borders of England. The strong castle of Roxburgh, which was the key of that country, had been five times taken by the English, and three times by the Scots, in less than seventeen months, and was then held by the gallant Lord Musgrave for Richard king of England.

Our worthy king had one daughter, of exquisite beauty and accomplishments; the flower of all Scotland, and her name was Margaret. This princess was courted by many of the principal nobility of the land, who all eagerly sought an alliance with the royal family, not only for the additional honour and power which it conferred on them and their posterity, but for the personal charms of the lady, which were of that high eminence, that no man could look on her without admiration. This emulation of the lords kept the court of King Robert full of bustle, homage, and splendour. All were anxious to frustrate the designs of their opponents, and to forward their own; so that high jealousies were often apparent in the sharp retorts, stern looks, and nodding plumes of the rival wooers; and as the princess had never disclosed her partiality for one above another, it was judged that Robert scarcely dared openly to give the preference to any of them. A circumstance, however, soon occurred, which brought the matter fairly to the test.

It happened on a lovely summer day, at the end of July, that three and twenty noble rivals for the hand of the beauteous princess were all assembled at the palace of Linlithgow; but the usual gaiety, mirth, and repartee did not prevail; for the king had received bad tidings that day, and he sat gloomy and sad.

Musgrave had issued from the castle of Roxburgh, had surprised the castle of Jedburgh, and taken prisoner William, brother to the lord of Galloway; slain many loyal Scottish subjects, and wasted Teviotdale with fire and sword. The conversation turned wholly on the state of affairs on the border, and the misery to which that country was exposed by the castle of Roxburgh remaining in the hands of the English; and at length the king enquired impatiently, how it came that Sir Philip Musgrave had surprised the castle this last time, when his subjects were so well aware of their danger.

The earl of Hume made answer, that it was wholly an affair of chivalry, and one of the bravest and noblest acts that ever was performed. Musgrave's mistress, the lady Jane Howard, of the blood royal, and the greatest heiress of the north of England, had refused to see him, unless he gained back his honour by the retaking of that perilous castle, and keeping it against all force, intercession, or guile, till the end of the Christmas holidays. That he had accomplished the former in the most gallant stile; and, from the measures that he had adopted, and the additional fortifications that he had raised, there was every possibility that he would achieve the latter.

"What," said the king, "must the spirit of chivalry then be confined to the country of our enemies? Have our noble dames of Scotland less heroism in their constitutions than those of the south? Have they fewer of the charms of beauty, or have their lovers less spirit to fulfil their commands? By this sceptre in my right hand, I will give my daughter, the princess Margaret, to the knight who shall take that castle of Roxburgh out of the hands of the English before the expiry of the Christmas holidays."

Every lord and knight was instantly on his feet to accept the proposal, and every one had his hand stretched towards the royal chair for audience, when Margaret arose herself, from the king's left hand, where she was seated, and flinging her left arm backward, on which swung a scarf of gold, and stretching her right, that gleamed with bracelets of rubies and diamonds, along the festive board, "Hold, my noble lords," said she; "I am too deeply interested here not to have a word to say. The grandchild of the great Bruce must not be given away to every adventurer without her own approval. Who among you will venture his honour and his life for me?" Every knight waved his right hand aloft and dashed it on the hilt of his sword, eyeing the graceful attitude and dignified form of the princess with rapture of delight. "It is well," continued she, "the spirit of chivalry *has not* deserted the Scottish nation—hear me then: My father's vow shall stand; I will give my hand in marriage to the knight who shall take that castle for the king, my father, before the expiry of the Christmas holidays, and rid our border of that nest of reavers; but with this proviso only, that, in case of his attempting and failing in the undertaking, he shall forfeit all his lands, castles, towns, and towers to me, which shall form part of my marriage-portion to his rival. Is it fit that the daughter of a king should be given up or won as circumstances may suit, or that the risk should all be on one side? Who would be so unreasonable as expect it? This, then, with the concurrence of my lord and father, is my determination, and by it will I stand."

The conditions were grievously hard, and had a damping and dismal effect on the courtly circle. The light of every eye deadened into a dim and sullen scowl. It was a deed that promised glory and renown to adventure their blood for such a dame,—to win such a lady as the Princess of Scotland: But, to give up their broad lands and castles to enrich a hated rival, was an obnoxious consideration, and what in all likelihood was to be the issue. When all the forces of the land had been unable to take the castle by storm, where was the probability that any of them was now to succeed? None accepted the conditions. Some remained silent; some shook their heads, and muttered incoherent mumblings; others strode about the room, as if in private consultation.

"My honoured liege," said Lady Margaret, "none of the lords or knights of your court have the spirit to accept of my conditions. Be pleased then to grant me a sufficient force. I shall choose the officers for them myself, and I engage to take the castle of Roxburgh before Christmas. I will disappoint the bloody Musgrave of his bride; and the world shall see whether the charms of Lady Jane Howard or those of Margaret Stuart shall rouse their admirers to deeds of the most desperate valour. Before the

Christmas bells have tolled, that shall be tried on the rocks, in the rivers, in the air, and the bowels of the earth. In the event of my enterprise proving successful, all the guerdon that I ask is, the full and free liberty of giving my hand to whom I will. It shall be to no one that is here." And so saying she struck it upon the table, and again took her seat at the king's left hand.

Every foot rung on the floor with a furious tramp, in unison with that stroke of the princess's hand. The taunt was not to be brooked. Nor was it. The haughty blood of the Douglasses could bear it no longer. James, the gallant earl of Douglas and Mar, stepped forward from the circle. "My honoured liege, and master," said he, "I have not declined the princess's offer,—beshrew my heart if ever it embraced such a purpose. But the stake is deep, and a moment's consideration excusable. I have considered, and likewise decided. I accept the lady's proposals. With my own vassals alone, and at my own sole charge, will I rescue the castle from the hands of our enemies, or perish in the attempt. The odds are high against me. But it is now a Douglas or a Musgrave: God prosper the bravest!"

"Spoken like yourself, noble Douglas," said the king, "The higher the stake the greater the honour. The task be yours, and may the issue add another laurel to the heroic name."

"James of Douglas," said Lady Margaret, "dost thou indeed accept of these hard conditions for my sake? Then the hand of thy royal mistress shall buckle on the armour in which thou goest to the field, but never shall unloose it, unless from a victor or a corse!" And with that she stretched forth her hand, which Douglas, as he kneeled with one knee on the ground, took and pressed to his lips.

Every one of the nobles shook Douglas by the hand, and wished him success. Does any man believe that there was one among them that indeed wished it? No, there was not a chief present that would not have rejoiced to have seen him led to the gallows. His power was too high already, and they dreaded that now it might be higher than ever: and, moreover, they saw themselves outdone by him in heroism, and felt degraded by the contract thus concluded.

The standard of the Douglas was reared, and the bloody heart flew far over many a lowland dale. The subordinate gentlemen rose with their vassals, and followed the banner of their chief; but the more powerful kept aloof, or sent ambiguous answers. They deemed the service undertaken little better than the frenzy of a madman.

There was at that time a powerful border baron, nicknamed Sir Ringan Redhough, by which name alone he was distinguished all the rest of his life. He was warden of the middle marches, and head of the most warlike and adventurous sept in all that country. The answer which this hero gave to his own cousin, Thomas Middlemas, who came to expostulate with him from Douglas, is still preserved verbatim: "What, man, are a' my brave lads to lie in bloody claes that the Douglas may lie i' snaw-white sheets wi' a bonny bedfellow? Will that keep the braid border for the king, my master? Tell him to keep their hands fu' an' their haunches toom, an' they'll soon be blythe to leave the lass an' loup at the ladle; an' the fient ae cloot shall cross the border to gar their pots play brown atween Dirdanhead and Cocket-fell. Tell him this, an' tell him that Redhough said it. If he dinna work by wiles he'll never pouch the profit. But if he canna do it, an' owns that he canna do it, let him send word to me, an' I'll tak' it for him."

With these words he turned his back, and abruptly left his cousin, who returned to Douglas, ill satisfied with the success of his message, but, nevertheless, delivered it faithfully. "That curst carle," said the Douglas, "is a thorn in my thigh, as well as a buckler on my arm. He's as cunning as a fox, as stubborn as an oak, and as fierce as a lion. I must temporize for the present, as I cannot do without his support, but the time may come that he may be humbled, and made to know his betters; since one endeavour has failed, we must try another, and, if that do not succeed, another still."

The day after that, as Sir Ringan was walking out at his own gate, an old man, with a cowl, and a long grey beard, accosted him. "May the great spirit of the elements shield thee, and be thy protector, knight," said he.

"An' wha may he be, carle, an it be your will?" said Ringan; "An' wha may ye be that gie me sic a sachless benediction? As to my shield and protection, look ye here!" and with that he touched his two-handed sword, and a sheaf of arrows that was swung at his shoulder; "an' what are all your saints and lang nebbit spirits to me?"

"It was a random salutation, knight," said the old man, seeing his mood and temper; "I am not a priest but a prophet. I come not to load you with blessings, curses, nor homilies, all equally unavailing, but to tell you what shall be in the times that are to come. I have had visions of futurity that have torn up the tendrils of my spirit by the roots. Would you like to know what is to befal you and your house in the times that are to come?"

"I never believe a word that you warlocks say," replied the knight; "but I like aye to hear what you *will* say about matters; though it is merely to laugh at ye, for I dinna gie credit to ane o' your predictions. Sin' the Rhymer's days, the spirit o' true warlockry is gane. He foretauld muckle that has turned out true; an' something that I hope *will* turn out true: But ye're a' bairns to him."

"Knight," said the stranger, "I can tell you more than ever the Rhymer conceived, or thought upon; and, moreover, I can explain the words of True Thomas, which neither you nor those to whom they relate in the smallest degree comprehend. Knowest thou the prophecy of the Hart and the Deer, as it is called?

'Quhere the hearte heavit in het blude over hill
    and howe,
There shall the dinke deire droule for the dowe:
Two fleite footyde maydenis shall tredde the greine,
And the mone and the starre shall flashe betweine.
Quhere the proude hiche halde and heveye hande
    beire
Ane frenauch shall feide on ane faderis frene feire,

In dinging at the starris the D shall doupe down,
But the S shall be S quhane the heide S is gone.' "

"I hae heard the reide often and often," said the knight, "but the
man's unborn that can understand that. Though the prophecies
and the legends of the Rhymer take the lead i' my lear, I hae
always been obliged to make that a passover."

"There is not one of all his sayings that relates as much to you
and your house, knight. It foretels that the arms of your family
shall supersede those of Douglas, which you know are the bloody
heart; and that in endeavouring to exalt himself to the stars, the D,
that is the Douglas, shall fall, but that your house and name shall
remain when the Stuarts are no more."

"By the horned beasts of Old England, my father's portion, and
my son's undiminished hope," exclaimed the knight,—"Thou art
a cunning man! I now see the bearing o' the prophecy as plainly as
I see the hill o' Mountcomyn before my e'e; and, as I know
Thomas never is wrong, I believe it. Now is the time, auld
warlock,—now is the time; he's ettling at a king's daughter, but
his neck lies in wad, and the forfeit will be his undoing."

"The time is not yet come, valiant knight; nevertheless the
prophecy is true. Has thy horse's hoof ever trode, or thine eye
journeyed, over the Nine Glens of Niddisdale?"

"I hae whiles gotten a glisk o' them."

"They are extensive, rich, and beautiful."

"They're nae less, auld carle; they're nae less. They can send
nine thousand leel men an' stout to the field in a pinch."

"It is recorded in the book of fate,—it is written there—"

"The devil it is, auld carle; that's mair than I thought o'."

"Hold thy peace: lay thine hand upon thy mouth, and be silent
till I explain: I say I have seen it in the visions of the night,—I have
seen it in the stars of heaven"—

"What? the Nine Glens o' Niddisdale amang the starns o'
heaven! by hoof and horn, it was rarely seen, warlock."

"I say that I have seen it,—they are all to belong to thy house."

94

"Niddisdale a' to pertain to my house!"

"All."

"Carle, I gie nae credit to sic forbodings; but I have heard something like this afore. Will ye stay till I bring my son Robin, the young Master of Mountcomyn, and let him hear it? For aince a man takes a mark on his way, I wadna hae him to tine sight o't. Mony a time has the tail o' the king's elwand pointed me the way to Cumberland; an' as often has the ee o' the Charlie-wain blinkit me hame again. A man's nae the waur o' a bit beacon o' some kind,—a bit of hope set afore him, auld carle; an' the Nine Glens o' Niddisdale are nae Willie-an-the-Wisp in a lad's ee."

"From Roxburgh castle to the tower of Sark,"—

"What's the auld-warld birkie saying?"

"From the Deadwater-fell to the Linns of Cannoby,—from the Linns of Cannoby to the heights of Manor and the Deucharswire,—shall thy son, and the representatives of thy house, ride on their own lands."

"May ane look at your foot, carle? Take off that huge wooden sandal, an it be your will."

"Wherefore should I knight?"

"Because I dread ye are either the devil or Master Michael Scott."

"Whoever I am, I am a friend to you and to yours, and have told you the words of truth. I have but one word more to say:— Act always in concert with the Douglasses, while they act in concert with the king your master,—not a day, nor an hour, nor a moment longer. It is thus, and thus alone, that you must rise and the Douglas fall. Remember the words of True Thomas,—

'Quhane the wingit hors at his maistere sal wince,
'Let wyse men cheat the chevysance.' "

"There is something mair about you than other folk, auld man. If ye be my kinsman, Michael Scott the warlock, I crave your pardon, Master; but if you are that dreadfu' carle–I mean that learned and wonderfu' man, why you are welcome to my castle.

But you are not to turn my auld wife into a hare, Master, an' hunt her up an' down the hills wi' my ain grews; nor my callants into naigs to scamper about on i' the night-time when they hae ither occupations to mind. There is naething i' my tower that isna at your command; for, troth, I wad rather brow a' the Ha's and the Howard's afore I beardit you."

"I set no foot in your halls, knight. This night is a night among many to me; and wo would be to me if any thing canopied my head save the cope of heaven. There are horoscopes to be read this night for a thousand years to come. One cake of your bread and one cup of your wine is all that the old wizard requests of you, and that he must have."

The knight turned back and led the seer into the inner-court, and fed him with bread and wine, and every good thing; but well he noted that he asked no holy benediction on them like the palmers and priors that wandered about the country; and, therefore, he had some lurking dread of the old man. He did not thank the knight for his courtesy, but, wiping his snowy beard, he turned abruptly away, and strode out at the gate of the castle. Sir Ringan kept an eye on him privately till he saw him reach the top of Blake Law, a small dark hill immediately above the castle. There he stopped and looked around him, and taking two green sods, he placed the one above the other, and laid himself down on his back, resting his head upon the two sods,—his body half raised, and his eyes fixed on heaven. The knight was almost frightened to look at him; but sliding into the cleuch, he ran secretly down to the tower to bring his lady to see this wonderful old warlock. When they came back he was gone, and no trace of him to be seen, nor saw they him any more at that time.

James Hogg, THE THREE PERILS OF MAN

*　　*　　*

In the nineteenth century the movement of Scotsmen through the world became pronounced and varied. Carlyle after his marriage moved to London.
Jane Welsh to Mrs Carlyle, Hoddam Hill:

Haddington, Wednesday, 'Spring 1826'
My dear Mrs. Carlyle—*Thomas* mentioned your wish to hear from me, more than two weeks since, and the intimation, I assure you, would have placed me at my writing-desk forthwith; but that it happened I had a cap for you just then on hand, which I somehow settled in my own mind *must* go along with the letter.—Now, I am by no means, the speediest needlewoman in the world, as you had ample opportunity of noticing while I sojourned at the Hill; and besides I have been unfitted for working

Jane Welsh Carlyle, from a miniature

97

at anything lately, but by starts, owing to an almost continual severe pain in my head: so that, all things considered, it is sufficiently intelligible how, with the best intentions, I should not have put the finishing stitch to this labour of love, till within the present hour. And what is it, after all my pains? Alas, that I have to fall on so paltry a shift to manifest my affectionate remembrance of you! Alas, that it has not pleased Fate to make me a powerful Queen, or even a powerful subject! Alas, finally, that the whole Universe is not ordered just according to my good pleasure!—It is better, you are thinking, as it is. Well! at bottom perhaps I think so too. But yet the wide discrepancy between my wishes and my powers will, at times, send a sharp pang through my heart, and tempt me to doubt, if *indeed* whatever is, be best.

Will you believe it, Mr. Carlyle has been within sixteen miles of me for three weeks, and we have not once seen each other's face! Now, is not this a pretty story? Can any one fancy a severer trial of patience? Positively, I am expecting to have my name transmitted to posterity along with the Patriarch Job's; for the *woman* who could undergo this thing, and yet not die of rage, could also survive, with a meek spirit, the carrying away of oxen and asses, the burning up of sheep, and even the smothering of sons and daughters. However, it seems probable he will speedily return for a longer period; and in the meantime, perhaps Fate may get into a more gracious humour: if she does not, I see nothing for it but to take the upper hand with her,—if we can.—Enter James Johnstone!—

Well! here is one thing settled to my heart's content; the Parish School is actually ours. Honest James was told the good news of his election, sitting by my side; and it would be difficult to say whether he or I was the happier. For, besides the pleasure which, I knew, this termination of the business would give to "*Somebody*," I have very good cause to be rejoiced at it upon my own account. Mr. Johnstone will be worth his weight of gold to me, in my present situation; I am so ill off for some one to talk to about— *Greek and Latin!*

Were the Shawbrae but come to as happy an issue I should take heart and think that "the wheel of my Destiny" had made a turn. But "where an equal poise of hope and fear does arbitrate the event, my nature is," that I incline to fear rather than hope. The Major will surely not keep us much longer in suspense. I must now write a few lines to Jean in return for her postscript. Remember me in the kindest manner to all the rest. Make much of Thomas now that you have got him back again. And never cease to think of *me* with affection. It will be long before I forget you or the time I passed beside you.

JANE WELSH.

P.S.—I will send a proper front for "my" caps when I go to Edinburgh; but there is no such thing to be got in this Royal Borough. A certain Barber in the place is the happy possessor of three red ones; a black one, I suppose, would have been too much. The muslin cap, you will perceive, has met with an accident behind, which I hope you will put up with on account of the excellence of my darning.

LETTER 5

At Templand, Tuesday, 17th October, 1826, we were wedded (in the quietest fashion devisable; Parish Minister, and except my Brother John, no other stranger present); and, directly after breakfast, drove off, on similar terms, for Comley Bank, Edinburgh; and arrived there that night. The following is a postscript to a Letter of mine.—T. C.

To Mrs. Carlyle, Scotsbrig.

21, Comley Bank, 9 Dec., 1826.

My dear Mother—I must not let this Letter go without adding *my* "be of good cheer." You would rejoice to see how much better my Husband is than when we came hither. And we are really very happy; and when he falls upon some work, we shall be still happier. Indeed I should be very stupid or very thankless, if I did not congratulate myself every hour of the day on the lot which it has pleased Providence to assign me. My Husband is so kind! so, in all respects, after my own heart! I was sick one day, and he nursed me as well as my own Mother could have done, and he never says a hard word to me—unless I richly deserve it. We see great numbers of people here, but are always most content alone. My Husband reads then, and I read or work, or just sit and look at him, which I really find as profitable an employment as any other. God bless you and my little Jean, whom I hope to see at no very distant date.

Ever affectionately yours,

JANE B. WELSH.

from NEW LETTERS AND MEMORIALS OF
JANE WELSH CARLYLE

*　　*　　*

In August 1829 there occurred the great floods in the Province of Moray and adjoining districts. Two years later Sir Thomas Dick Lauder, spurred on by Sir Henry Cockburn of Bonaly, Advocate, published his Account of the Great Floods which would have done credit to a Namier or Cobb. It is a small masterpiece of a sociological study combining scientific detail with comment gleaned from first-hand witnesses.

The flood, both in the Spey and its tributary burn, was terrible at the village of Charlestown of Aberlour. On the 3d of August, Charles Cruickshanks, the innkeeper, had a party of friends in his house. There was no inebriety, but there was a fiddle; and what Scotsman is he who does not know, that the well jerked strains of a lively strathspey have a potent spell in them that goes beyond even the witchery of the bowl? On one who daily inhales the breezes from the musical stream that gives name to the measure, the influence is powerful, and it was that day felt by Cruickshanks with a more than ordinary degree of excitement. He was joyous to a pitch that made his wife grave. I have already noticed the predestinarian principles prevalent in these parts. Mrs Cruickshanks was deeply affected by her husband's unusual jollity. "Surely my goodman is daft the day," said she gravely, "I ne'er saw him dance at sic a rate. Lord grant that he binna *fey!*"

When the river began to rise rapidly in the evening, Cruickshanks, who had a quantity of wood lying near the mouth of the burn, asked two of his neighbours, James Stewart and James Mackerran, to go and assist him in dragging it out of the water. They readily complied, and Cruickshanks, getting on the loose raft of wood, they followed him, and did what they could in pushing and hauling the pieces of timber ashore, till the stream increased so much, that, with one voice, they declared they would stay no longer, and, making a desperate effort, they plunged over head, and reached the land with the greatest difficulty. They then tried all their eloquence to persuade Cruickshanks to come away, but he was a bold and experienced floater, and laughed at their fears; nay, so utterly reckless was he, that, having now diminished the crazy ill-put-together raft he stood on, till it consisted of a few spars only, he employed himself in trying to catch at and save some hay-cocks belonging to the clergyman, which were floating past him. But, while his attention was so engaged, the flood was rapidly increasing, till, at last, even his dauntless heart appalled at its magnitude and fury. "A horse! A horse!" he loudly and anxiously cried, "Run for one of the minister's horses, and ride in with a rope, else I must go with the stream." He was quickly obeyed, but ere a horse arrived, the flood had rendered it impossible to approach him.

Seeing that he must abandon all hope of help in that way, Cruickshanks was now seen, as if summoning up all his resolution and presence of mind, to make the perilous attempt of dashing through the raging current, with his frail and imperfect raft.

Grasping more firmly the iron shod pole he held in his hand, called in floater's language a *sting*, he pushed resolutely into it; but he had hardly done so, when the violence of the water wrenched from his hold that which was all he had to depend on. A shriek burst from his friends, as they beheld the wretched raft dart off with him, down the stream, like an arrow freed from the bow-string. But the mind of Cruickshanks was no common one to quail before the first approach of danger. He poised himself, and stood balanced, with determination and self-command in his eye, and no sound of fear, or of complaint, was heard to come from him. At the point where the burn met the river, in the ordinary state of both, there grew some trees, now surrounded by deep and strong currents, and far from the land. The raft took a direction towards one of these, and seeing the wide and tumultuous waters of the Spey before him, in which there was no hope that his loosely connected logs could stick one moment together, he coolly prepared himself, and, collecting all his force into one well timed and well directed effort, he sprang, caught a tree, and clung among its boughs, whilst the frail raft hurried away from under his foot, was dashed into fragments, and scattered on the bosom of the waves. A shout of joy arose from his anxious friends, for they now deemed him safe; but *he* uttered no shout in return. Every nerve was strained to procure help. "A boat!" was the general cry, and some ran this way and some that, to endeavour to procure one. It was now between 7 and 8 o'clock in the evening. A boat was speedily obtained from Mr Gordon of Aberlour, and, though no one there was very expert in its use, it was quickly manned by people, eager to save Cruickshanks from his perilous situation. The current was too terrible about the tree, to admit of their nearing it, so as to take him directly into the boat; but their object was to row through the smoother water, to such a distance as might enable them to throw a rope to him, by which means they hoped to drag him to the boat. Frequently did they attempt this, and as frequently were they foiled, even by that which was considered as the gentler part of the stream, for it hurried them past the point whence they wished to make the cast of their rope, and compelled them to row up again by the side, to start on each fresh adventure. Often were they carried so much in the direction of the tree, as to be compelled to exert all their strength to pull themselves away from him they would have saved, that they might avoid the vortex that would have caught and swept them to destruction. And often was poor Cruickshanks tantalized with the approach of help, which came but to add, to the other miseries of his situation, that of the bitterest disappointment. Yet he bore all calmly. In the transient glimpses they had of him, as they were driven past him, they saw no blenching on his dauntless countenance,—they heard no reproach, no complaint, no sound, but an occasional short exclamation of encouragement to persevere in their friendly endeavours. But the evening wore on, and still they were unsuccessful. It seemed to them that something more than mere natural causes was operating against them. "His hour is come!" said they, as they regarded one another with looks of awe; "our struggles are vain." The courage and the hope which had hitherto supported them began to fail, and the descending shades of night extinguished the last feeble sparks of both, and put an end to their endeavours.

Fancy alone can picture the horrors that must have crept on the unfortunate man, as, amidst the impenetrable darkness which now prevailed, he became aware of the continued increase of the flood that roared around him, by its gradual advance towards his feet, whilst the rain and the tempest continued to beat more and more dreadfully upon him. That these were long ineffectual in shaking his collected mind, we know from the fact, afterwards ascertained, that he actually wound up his watch while in this dreadful situation. But, hearing no more the occasional passing exclamations of those who had been hitherto trying to succour him, he began to shout for help in a voice that became every moment more long drawn and piteous, as, between the gusts of the tempest, and borne over the thunder of the waters, it fell from time to time on the ears of his clustered friends, and rent the heart of his distracted wife. Ever and anon it came, and hoarser than before, and there was an occasional wildness in its note, and now and then a strange and clamorous repetition for a time, as if despair had inspired him with an unnatural energy. But the shouts became gradually shorter,—less audible, and less frequent,—till at last their eagerly listening ears could catch them no longer. "Is he gone?"—was the half-whispered question they put to one another, and the smothered responses that were muttered around but too plainly told how much the fears of all were in unison.

"What was that?" cried his wife in delirious scream,—"That was his whistle I heard!"—She said truly. A shrill whistle, such as that which is given with the fingers in the mouth, rose again over the loud din of the deluge, and the yelling of the storm. He was not yet gone. His voice was but cracked by his frequent exertions to make it heard, and he had now resorted to an easier mode of transmitting to his friends the certainty of his safety. For some time his unhappy wife drew hope from such considerations, but his whistles, as they came more loud and prolonged, pierced the ears of his foreboding friends like the ill-omened cry of some warning spirit; and, it may be matter of question whether all believed that the sounds they heard were really mortal. Still they came louder and clearer for a brief space; but at last they were heard no more, save in his frantic wife's fancy, who continued to start as if she still heard them, and to wander about, and to listen, when all but herself were satisfied that she could never hear them again.

Wet, and weary, and shivering with cold, was this miserable woman, when the tardy dawn of morning beheld her, straining her eye-balls through the imperfect light, towards the trees where Cruickshanks had been last seen. There was something there that looked like the figure of a man, and on that her eyes fixed. But those around her saw, alas! too well, that what she fondly supposed to be her husband was but a bunch of wreck, gathered by the flood into one of the trees, for the one to which he clung had been swept away.

The body of poor Cruickshanks was found in the afternoon of next day on the Haugh of Dandaleith, some 4 or 5 miles below. As it had ever been his uniform practice to wind up his watch at night, and as it was discovered to be nearly full wound when it was taken from his pocket, the fact of his having had self-possession enough to obey his usual custom, under circumstances so terrible, is as unquestionable as it is wonderful. It had stopt at a quarter of an hour past 11 o'clock, which would seem to fix that as the fatal moment when the tree was rent away, for when that happened, his struggles amidst the raging waves of the Spey must have been few and short. When the men, who had so unsuccessfully attempted to save him, were talking over the matter, and agreeing that no human help could have availed him, "I'm thinkin' I could ha' ta'en him oot," said a voice in the circle. All eyes were turned towards the speaker, and a general expression of contempt followed, for it was a boy of the name of John Rainey, a reputed idiot, from the foot of Belrinnes, who spoke. "You!" cried a dozen voices at once, "what would you have done, you wise man?"—"I wud ha'e tied an empty anker-cask to the end o' a lang lang tow, an' I wud ha'e floated it aff frae near aboot whar the raft was ta'en first awa', an' syne, ye see, as the stream teuk the raft till the tree, maybe she wud ha'e ta'en the cask there too,—an' if Charley Cruickshanks had ance gotten a haud o' the rope,"—He would have finished, but his auditors were gone. They had silently slunk away in different directions, one man alone having muttered, as he went, something about "wisdom coming out the mouths of fools."

Sir Thomas Dick Lauder, AN ACCOUNT OF THE
GREAT FLOODS

*   *   *

The Member was written in 1831, and has been called the first political novel in English. It is about a Scot returned home, like many after him, wealthy from service in Bengal with the East

India Company. Archibald Jobbry tastes parliament and patronage:

It is surely a very extraordinary thing to observe at the meeting of every new Parliament how it is composed; but nothing is so much so as the fact that there is a continual increase of Scotchmen, which is most consolatory to all good subjects. Both England and Ireland have many boroughs represented by Scotchmen, but never yet has it been necessary for Scotland to bring a member out of either of these two nations. This, no doubt, is a cause of her prosperity, quite as much as the Union, of which so much is said, and proves the great utility of her excellent system of parish schools.

The remark occurred to me on the night of the first debate, when I looked round the House and saw of whom it consisted; and I said to a friend near me, before the address was moved, that it was a satisfactory sight to see so many very decent men assembled for the good of the nation; and it was an earnest to me that we would have on that night a more judicious division than for many years past. And, accordingly, it was so, for the King's Ministers had cooked their dish with great skill: no ingredient was in that could well be objected to, and it passed unanimously; so that my principles were put to no strain in doing as the other members did. The next important debate was concerning a matter in which some underling of office took upon him to meddle with an election; and, as I don't much approve of such doings, I resolved, though it was a Government question, to vote against Ministers, and to shew, on the first occasion, that I was independent of Lord Dilldam.

The question itself was of no great consequence, nor a single vote either way of much value; but it was an opportunity to place myself on a right footing with Ministers: indeed, after the cost that I had been at for my election, it was not pleasant to think that Lord Dilldam was to get all the credit of sending me into

106

Parliament, and my share of the public patronage likewise. Accordingly, to the very visible consternation of the Secretary of State for the Home Department, the Chancellor of the Exchequer, and two young Lords of the Treasury, who were in a great passion, being rash youths, I was found in the patriotic band of the minority. To be sure they said nothing direct to me, but I could discern that they spoke with their eyes; nevertheless, I was none afraid, and resolved to wait the upshot, which I had not long to do; for, in the course of two days, I received a letter begging my interest for Tom Brag, of Frailtown, who had applied to Lord Dilldam for a particular place, but whom his lordship had declined to assist, having promised to give his patronage to another. As Tom had been useful to me in the election, I was, of course, disposed to serve him; and, moreover, I was glad of such an early opportunity to convince Lord Dilldam that I was not to be counted one of his neck-and-heelers. So I went straight to the Secretary of State for the Home Department, and requested that he would let Tom Brag have the place, which he said he would be very happy to do; but he was greatly surprised at the way in which I had voted the other night, Lord Dilldam's members being always considered as among the firmest supporters of Government.

'That,' quo' I, 'may be very true; I am not, however, one of his, but standing on my own pockneuk: the rule does not apply to me. There is no doubt that I am naturally well-disposed towards his Majesty's ministers, but I must have a freedom of conscience in giving my votes. If you will give the lad Tom Brag this bit postie, I will not forget the favour,—giff for gaff is fair play, and you will find I observe it.'

The Minister looked at me with a queer, comical, piercing eye, and smiled; whereupon I inquired if my young man would have the post.

'It will be proper,' replied the Secretary, 'before I give you a definitive answer, that I should have time to investigate the matter.'

'No doubt,' said I; 'but if the place is not promised away, will my friend get it?'

'That's a very home question, Mr Jobbry.'

'It's my plain way, Mr. Secretary; and as the place is but a small matter, surely you might give me the promise without much hesitation.'

'Yes, Mr Jobbry, that is easily done; but do you know if it would please Lord Dilldam that we gave it to you.'

'I'll be very evendown with you: as an honest man, Mr Secretary, I cannot take it on me to say that the appointment of Tom Brag would give heartfelt satisfaction to his lordship; but I have set my mind on getting the place for Tom; and really, Mr Secretary, you must permit me to think that it's not just proper that an independent member should be refused a civil answer until my lord this or that has been consulted.'

'I beg your pardon, Mr Jobbry. I hope that you have no cause to think I have been uncivil: a system of conciliation and firmness belongs to Ministers on all occasions.'

'True, true,' said I: 'so Lord Sidmouth said would be the conduct of his ministry towards France, and then he went to war with them. But even, Mr Secretary, although you may go to war with me in your conciliation and firmness, as I consider a refusal in this matter would be, it will make no difference in the ordinary questions in Parliament; but you know that, from time to time, the Opposition make harassing motions, in which the good of the nation has no concern, though the felicity of Ministers may. You understand.'

'Really,' replied the Secretary of State, laughing, 'you are a very extraordinary man, Mr Jobbry.'

'I am an honest member of Parliament.'

'I see you are,' was the reply.

'Then if you do, Mr Secretary, you will promise me the place.'

In short, from less to more, I did not leave him till I got the promise; and from that time I heard no more of my Lord Dilldam.

I have been the more particular in this recital, as it was the first occasion on which I had to vindicate my independence; and it was well for me that I did it in a manner so very complete, for soon after there was a change of administration; and had I not done as I did, I must have gone to the right about, and lost every benefit and advantage that induced me to leave my pleasant country improvements in Scotland, to stew myself at the midnight hour with the cantrips of the House of Commons.

But, though this affair was not without the solace of a satisfaction, it was rather an inroad on my system; for, as my object in procuring a seat was to benefit my kith and kin, and to stick a harmless feather in my own cap, I was not quite content to give my patronage to a stranger. Thomas Brag had, no doubt, a claim upon me, and I very readily acknowledged it, especially as it helped to shew me in my true colours; but it would have been far more congenial to my principles had I got the post for a son of my own cousin, whom it would have fitted to a hair. But men in public life, and trafficking with affairs of state, must not expect every thing their own way; so I said nothing, but pocketed the loss, and pruned my wing for another flight, like the hawk in his jesses.

John Galt, THE MEMBER

*   *   *

Two great movements of Scots occur in the nineteenth century. During the persecution of the Covenanters in the seventeenth century, many Scots families had moved to Northern Ireland, and now were turning towards the Scots universities, particularly Glasgow.

Again, there was increasing dialogue between Scottish scientists and Cambridge University, the centre of scientific research in the country. At the age of seventeen, William Thomson left Glasgow University and entered St Peter's College, Cambridge. Ten years earlier his father had returned from Belfast to the Chair of Mathematics at Glasgow University. After five years at Cambridge, William Thomson was unanimously elected to the Chair of Natural Philosophy in Glasgow University in September 1846. He was only twenty-two, and was to remain with the University for the rest of his life: in time he became Lord Kelvin. There can be few scientists who matched the span of his insights as he moved from observation, to theory, to practice.

The Sounding Machine has done much to make navigation safer and easier. Formerly it was necessary to stop to take a sounding. Lord Kelvin, however, discarded rope for the sounding-lead, and used piano wire, provided with a device which gave the depth by showing the pressure of the air in a tube. Thus soundings can be obtained when proceeding at full speed.

A friend finding him surrounded with piano wire asked what sound he was trying to produce. 'The deep C,' was the quick reply.

Lord Kelvin's tidal machines were very wonderful; by them he could tell the time of high water, and the depth of tide water at any moment at any given place.

Many years were spent studying tides and waves; waves indeed occupied his thoughts all his life, because they run their course through all science and nature; and at all times he was observing and learning, and finding something new about them, even in the most ordinary occurrences. Once when a large company of us were breakfasting at Netherhall and he was quietly stirring his cup, he suddenly looked up and exclaimed with delight: 'This is remarkable. I have never seen these waves before'; then, jumping up, he went round the whole table, cup in hand, showing to each of us the way in which by moving his spoon in a certain manner a certain result followed.

Watching the ripples caused by the ducks at Netherhall was also a source of great interest to him. In a letter to Lord Rayleigh he said: 'We saw a fine mode of generating a regular procession of ring-waves in water. We were watching a set of ducks yesterday on our arrival here, and the beautiful echelons of waves which they made when swimming. They seemed pleased at being noticed, and one after another stopped swimming and called out to us in their own language. . . . By looking at the ring-waves we could count the number of quacks we had heard.'

William Thomson, Lord Kelvin, at the age of sixteen

He loved nature, but not as an artist

One of Lord Kelvin's lectures at the British Association was on 'The Physical Explanation of the Mackerel Sky.' He loved nature, but it was not as an artist. The sky was to him a lesson book, and the roar of the sea and the murmuring ripple of the Highland burn told him their secrets of motion and wave, while the mountains spoke of the age of the earth and past upheavals. I had a stiff argument with him once at the Royal Academy about art. I was very anxious he should admire a beautiful picture of Glen Sannox, with mist resting among the mountains; but he remarked that it was an unfortunate time to choose, and the artist ought to have waited till the mist had cleared away, and all the outlines of the mountains were distinctly seen. I tried to point out the artistic beauty of the picture, and also of another, a misty sunset, but he insisted that in so far as clouds or mists veiled the character of the landscape they were flaws. Some of his remarks, however, were very useful to me afterwards—he pointed out how beautiful geological lines were, and how utterly incorrectness in some of the pictures destroyed the effect. It made me realise the importance of a knowledge of geology to an artist, and that it is quite as necessary as anatomy.

The Atlantic Cable

It was my uncle's instruments that made long-distance telegraphy possible. Till he grasped the subject, a cable to America was looked upon as 'a mad dream.' The one idea of cable work was to get more and more powerful instruments to force the message through a cable, but it was not possible to get a cable which could endure such strong currents as were required for considerable distances. Lord Kelvin, on the other hand, brought his mind to bear upon an instrument which should be able to respond to the faintest possible electric current. The mirror-galvanometer was the result. Inside, a tiny magnet made of watch-spring is attached to the back of a minute convex mirror, the whole weighing only a grain and a half, and it is hung in the centre of a coil of very fine wire. A lamp directed on the mirror reflects a tiny spot of light on a scale, and as the electric current deflects the magnet, so the light moves to right or left, and the message is carried in Morse.

I think this was my uncle's pet instrument. I remember that it accompanied him on several visits, and being told how wonderful it was, and that I must not shake the table or run about near it.

To me it had a special interest because of learning that my uncle's little dog, Fairy, supplied from his coat the delicate fibre which suspended the mirror, my uncle having been unable to find anything else fine enough for the purpose. Once, when he was staying with us, the fibre broke, and he was in great difficulty till I produced one of my silkworm cocoons, and wound off some of the silk. To my immense gratification it proved exactly what was wanted, and after this I had the delight of being applied to regularly by my uncle for fresh supplies. It also came in useful for several other instruments; moreover, cocoon silk is still used for such purposes.

Watching the spot of light was a great strain; also there was a liability to mistakes; so Lord Kelvin's busy brain devised the Syphon Pen, by which the cable wrote its own messages. The pen was made of hair-like glass tubing; it did not touch the strip of paper which was mechanically carried past, but a little instrument, called the mouse-mill, electrified the ink and forced it in a fine spray through the pen.

It was most interesting to watch my uncle when bringing his invention to perfection, with his skilled hands deftly manipulating the delicate tubing, and bending it into shape with the heat from a lighted match.

The wonderful dexterity with which Lord Kelvin and Professor James Thomson were able to carry out their inventions was due greatly to their wise father, who had provided them with accommodation and conveniences when they were mere children, and encouraged them to make things for themselves instead of supplying them with ready-made toys.

The Mirror-Galvanometer was superseded by the Syphon Pen for submarine telegraphy, but the galvanometer is still one of the most useful instruments in the laboratory, and it was of immense value during the war to locate submarines and other vessels, and to tell the direction in which they were going. A cable in a zigzag pattern was laid over the bottom of the sea, and as an iron or steel vessel passed over any part of it, the mirror in the galvanometer, safely lodged and carefully watched at home, was deflected and gave up the secrets of the deep.

The laying of the first cable to America was a matter of overwhelming excitement. On 29th May 1858 the expedition started. My uncle was almost the last man on board. His all-important galvanometer had not arrived yet—would it come in time? Its construction had only been begun a fortnight before—was it ready? He paced up and down, watching and waiting in a state of intense anxiety: at last to his joy Donald MacFarlane, his assistant, arrived by express with a small object like a brass pot standing on four legs, and put it in his hands—the Mirror-Galvanometer!

Charles Bright, afterwards knighted for this work, had been entrusted with the making and the packing in of the cable. Little does the ordinary individual understand what such work involves. In the construction of the first Atlantic cable 340,500 miles of fine wire were used, enough to go thirteen times round the world, and considerably more than would be needed to reach the moon! The whole of a cable in process of construction must be tested from end to end to see that there is not a single flaw; then it has to be packed in the hold of the vessel. This last is a matter of great concern and difficulty. Unfortunately a terrible storm was met with not far from home, and the cable was seriously displaced and damaged. My mother has often told me of the awful suspense lest the vessel had gone down when, after the storm, the cable ceased speaking. It is impossible to realise the tension and, to use Lord Kelvin's words, 'harrowing anxiety' on board; no one seemed to breathe freely. A diary written at the time by the late Nicolas Wood, speaks of 'Dr. Thomson, in a perfect fever of nervous excitement, shaking like an aspen leaf, yet in mind clear and collected, testing and waiting with a half-despairing look for the result. . . . Mr. Bright looking to the professor for advice. . . .

Round the door crowded the sailors of the watch, peeping over each other's shoulders. . . . The eyes of all were directed to the instruments, watching for the slightest quiver indicative of life. Such a scene was never witnessed save at the bedside of the dying. . . . We looked at each other in silence. . . . Suddenly one sang out "Halloa! the spot has gone up to 40 degrees." The clerk at the ordinary instrument bolted right out of the room, scarcely knowing where he went for joy, and cried out: "Mr. Thomson! the cable's all right." Our joy was so deep and earnest it did not suffer us to speak for some seconds. . . . Never was more anxiety compressed into such a space. . . . The only instrument that kept us from despair was Dr. Thomson's. . . . On the night of 3rd August we got into shallow water. About ten Dr. Thomson came into the electrical cabin, evidently in a state of enjoyment so intense as to absorb his whole soul. . . . He then proceeded to congratulate those present on being connected with such an expedition.'

At last the great task was accomplished and the American end landed, ladies, unmindful of tar on their white hands and gloves, helping to haul it ashore. America went almost mad with joy when, on the ever memorable 5th of August 1858, the message rang across the Atlantic—

'Europe and America are united by telegraphic communication. Glory to God in the Highest, on earth peace, good will towards men.'

The injury, however, had been great, and the cable gradually ceased to work; but the fact had been definitely proved that a practicable cable could be laid to America, and later, in 1866, the task was accomplished, and telegraphic communication with America secured—not, however, without the most strenuous efforts on Lord Kelvin's part.

Agnes Gardner King, KELVIN THE MAN

*   *   *

It is a paradox that while Scotland in the nineteenth century aped English society, reflecting an unnatural snobbishness and class-consciousness, the benefits of the Union were being reflected in ever-widening spheres. In medicine the teaching hospitals of Edinburgh and Glasgow established close relations with their equivalents in London. And while domestic, and childish, differences between surgeons and medical men existed, invention thrived. On 10 March 1847, Sir James Simpson communicated a paper on Chloroform to the Medico-Chirurgical Society of Edinburgh:

"From the time at which I first saw ether-inhalation successfully practised in January last, I have had the conviction impressed upon my mind, that we would ultimately find that other therapeutic agents were capable of being introduced with equal rapidity and success into the system, through the same extensive and powerful channel of pulmonary absorption. . . .

"With various professional friends, more conversant with chemistry than I am, I have, since that time, taken opportunities of talking over the idea which I entertained of the probable existence or discovery of new therapeutic agents, capable of being introduced into the system by respiration, and the possibility of producing for inhalation vaporizable or volatile preparations of some of our more active and old-established medicines: and I have had, during the summer and autumn, ethereal tinctures, etc., of several potent drugs, manufactured for me, for experiment, by Messrs. Duncan, Flockhart, and Co., the excellent chemists and druggists of this city.

"Latterly, in order to avoid, if possible, some of the inconveniences and objections pertaining to sulphuric ether (particularly its disagreeable and very persistent smell, its occasional tendency to irritation of the bronchi during its first inspirations, and the large quantity of it occasionally required to be used, more especially in protracted cases of labour), I have tried upon myself and others the inhalation of different other volatile fluids, with the hope that some one of them might be found to possess the advantages of ether, without its disadvantages. . . .

"Chloroform was first discovered and described at nearly the same time by Soubeiran (1831), and Liebig (1832); its composition was first accurately ascertained by the distinguished French chemist, Dumas, in 1835. . . .

"It is a dense, limpid, colourless liquid, readily evaportaing, and possessing an agreeable, fragrant, fruit-like odour, and a saccharine pleasant taste.

"As an inhaled anæsthetic agent, it possesses over sulphuric ether the following advantages:—

"1. A greatly less quantity of chloroform than of ether is requisite to produce the anæsthetic effect; usually from a hundred to a hundred and twenty drops of chloroform only being sufficient; and with some patients much less. I have seen a strong person rendered completely insensible by six or seven inspirations of thirty drops of the liquid.

"2. Its action is much more rapid and complete, and generally more persistent. I have almost always seen from ten to twenty full inspirations suffice. Hence the time of the surgeon is saved; and that preliminary stage of excitement, which pertains to all narcotizing agents, being curtailed, or indeed practically abolished, the patient has not the same degree of tendency to exhilaration and talking.

"3. Most of those who know from previous experience the sensations produced by ether inhalation, and who have subsequently breathed the chloroform, have strongly declared the inhalation and influence of chloroform to be far more agreeable and pleasant than those of ether.

"4. I believe, that considering the small quantity requisite, as compared with ether, the use of chloroform will be less expensive than that of ether; more especially, as there is every prospect that the means of forming it may be simplified and cheapened.

"5. Its perfume is not unpleasant, but the reverse; and the

odour of it does not remain, for any length of time, obstinately attached to the clothes of the attendant,—or exhaling in a disagreeable form from the lungs of the patient, as so generally happens with sulphuric ether.

"6. Being required in much less quantity, it is much more portable and transmissible than sulphuric ether.

"7. No special kind of inhaler or instrument is necessary for its exhibition. A little of the liquid diffused upon the interior of a hollow-shaped sponge, or a pocket-handkerchief, or a piece of linen or paper, and held over the mouth and nostrils, so as to be fully inhaled, generally suffices in about a minute or two to produce the desired effect." . . .

After referring in detail to the chemical constitution of chloroform, he adds:—

"It is perhaps not unworthy of remark, that when Soubeiran, Liebig, and Dumas engaged, a few years back, in those inquiries and experiments by which the formation and composition of chloroform was first discovered, their sole and only object was the investigation of a point in philosophical chemistry. They laboured for the pure love and extension of knowledge. They had no idea that the substance to which they called the attention of their chemical brethren could or would be turned to any *practical* purpose, or that it possessed any physiological or therapeutic effects upon the animal economy. I mention this to show, that the *cui bono* argument against philosophical investigations, on the ground that there may be at first no apparent practical benefit to be derived from them, has been amply refuted in this, as it has been in many other instances. For I feel assured, that the use of chloroform will soon entirely supersede the use of ether; and, from the facility and rapidity of its exhibition, it will be employed as an anæsthetic agent in many cases, and under many circumstances, in which ether would never have been had recourse to. Here then we have a substance which, in the first instance, was merely interesting as a matter of scientific curiosity and research, becoming rapidly an object of intense importance,

118

as an agent by which human suffering and agony may be annulled and abolished, under some of the most trying circumstances in which human nature is ever placed.

"Since the above observations were sent to the press, I have—through the great kindness of Professor Miller and Dr. Duncan—had an opportunity of trying the effects of the inhalation of chloroform, to-day, in three cases of operation in the Royal Infirmary of Edinburgh. A great collection of professional gentlemen and students witnessed the results, and among the number was Professor Dumas of Paris, the chemist who first ascertained and established the chemical composition of chloroform. He happened to be passing through Edinburgh, engaged along with Dr. Milne Edwards, who accompanied him, in an official investigation for the French Government,—and was, in no small degree, rejoiced to witness the wonderful physiological effects of a substance with whose chemical history his own name was so intimately connected.

J. Duns, MEMOIR OF SIR J. Y. SIMPSON BART

*   *   *

The 1848 revolution in Europe when currencies went wild affected the economy of Scotland deeply. On 17 May 1848 the family of Andrew Carnegie left Dunfermline bound for Glasgow on their way to America.

Pittsburgh and Work

The great question now was, what could be found for me to do. I had just completed my thirteenth year, and I fairly panted to get to work that I might help the family to a start in the new land. The prospect of want had become to me a frightful nightmare. My thoughts at this period centered in the determination that we

119

should make and save enough of money to produce three hundred dollars a year—twenty-five dollars monthly, which I figured was the sum required to keep us without being dependent upon others. Every necessary thing was very cheap in those days.

The brother of my Uncle Hogan would often ask what my parents meant to do with me, and one day there occurred the most tragic of all scenes I have ever witnessed. Never can I forget it. He said, with the kindest intentions in the world, to my mother, that I was a likely boy and apt to learn; and he believed that if a basket were fitted out for me with knickknacks to sell, I could peddle them around the wharves and make quite a considerable sum. I never knew what an enraged woman meant till then. My mother was sitting sewing at the moment, but she sprang to her feet with outstretched hands and shook them in his face.

"What! my son a peddler and go among rough men upon the wharves! I would rather throw him into the Allegheny River. Leave me!" she cried, pointing to the door, and Mr. Hogan went.

She stood a tragic queen. The next moment she had broken down, but only for a few moments did tears fall and sobs come. Then she took her two boys in her arms and told us not to mind her foolishness. There were many things in the world for us to do and we could be useful men, honored and respected, if we always did what was right. It was a repetition of Helen Macgregor, in her reply to Osbaldistone in which she threatened to have her prisoners "chopped into as many pieces as there are checks in the tartan." But the reason for the outburst was different. It was not because the occupation suggested was peaceful labor, for we were taught that idleness was disgraceful; but because the suggested occupation was somewhat vagrant in character and not entirely respectable in her eyes. Better death. Yes, mother would have taken her two boys, one under each arm, and perished with them rather than they should mingle with low company in their extreme youth.

As I look back upon the early struggles this can be said: there was not a prouder family in the land. A keen sense of honor,

120

independence, self-respect, pervaded the household. Walter Scott said of Burns that he had the most extraordinary eye he ever saw in a human being. I can say as much for my mother. As Burns has it:

> "Her eye even turned on empty space,
> Beamed keen with honor."

Anything low, mean, deceitful, shifty, coarse, underhand, or gossipy was foreign to that heroic soul. Tom and I could not help growing up respectable characters, having such a mother and such a father, for the father, too, was one of nature's noblemen, beloved by all, a saint. . . .

My brother and Mr. Phipps conducted the iron business so successfully that I could leave for weeks at a time without anxiety. There was danger lest I should drift away from the manufacturing to the financial and banking business. My successes abroad brought me tempting opportunities, but my preference was always for manufacturing. I wished to make something tangible and sell it and I continued to invest my profits in extending the works at Pittsburgh.

The small shops put up originally for the Keystone Bridge Company had been leased for other purposes and ten acres of ground had been secured in Lawrenceville on which new and extensive shops were erected. Repeated additions to the Union Iron Mills had made them the leading mills in the United States for all sorts of structural shapes. Business was promising and all the surplus earnings I was making in other fields were required to expand the iron business. I had become interested, with my friends of the Pennsylvania Railroad Company, in building some railways in the Western States, but gradually withdrew from all such enterprises and made up my mind to go entirely contrary to the adage not to put all one's eggs in one basket. I determined that the proper policy was "to put all good eggs in one basket and then watch that basket." . . .

I believe the true road to pre-eminent success in any line is to make yourself master in that line. I have no faith in the policy of

121

scattering one's resources, and in my experience I have rarely if ever met a man who achieved pre-eminence in money-making—certainly never one in manufacturing—who was interested in many concerns. The men who have succeeded are men who have chosen one line and stuck to it. It is surprising how few men appreciate the enormous dividends derivable from investment in their own business. There is scarcely a manufacturer in the world who has not in his works some machinery that should be thrown out and replaced by improved appliances; or who does not for the want of additional machinery or new methods lose more than sufficient to pay the largest dividend obtainable by investment beyond his own domain. And yet most business men whom I have known invest in bank shares and in far-away enterprises, while the true gold mine lies right in their own factories.

I have tried always to hold fast to this important fact. It has been with me a cardinal doctrine that I could manage my own capital better than any other person, much better than any board of directors. The losses men encounter during a business life which seriously embarrass them are rarely in their own business, but in enterprises of which the investor is not master. My advice to young men would be not only to concentrate their whole time and attention on the one business in life in which they engage, but to put every dollar of their capital into it. If there be any business that will not bear extension, the true policy is to invest the surplus in first-class securities which will yield a moderate but certain revenue if some other growing business cannot be found. As for myself my decision was taken early. I would concentrate upon the manufacture of iron and steel and be master in that.

Andrew Carnegie, from his autobiography

*   *   *

The discovery of Africa was a carrot for Christian mission. The whole kingdom rejoiced in it. To save the soul of the heathen was a pearl to be treasured and there seemed no discrepancy if it was acquired under a banner with commerce and the Bible. There were, of course, diversions from saving grace—into health and education. David Livingstone was in what we now know as Zambia in the year 1855:

I resolved on the following day to visit the falls of Victoria, called by the natives Mosioatunya, or more anciently Shongwe. Of these we had often heard since we came into the country: indeed one of the questions asked by Sebituane was, "Have you smoke that sounds in your country?" They did not go near enough to examine them, but, viewing them with awe at a distance, said, in reference to the vapour and noise, "Mosi oa tunya" (smoke does sound there). It was previously called Shongwe, the meaning of which I could not ascertain. The word for a "pot" resembles this, and it may mean a seething caldron; but I am not certain of it. Being persuaded that Mr. Oswell and myself were the very first Europeans who ever visited the Zambesi in the centre of the country, and that this is the connecting link between the known and unknown portions of that river, I decided to use the same liberty as the Makololo did, and gave the only English name I have affixed to any part of the country. No better proof of previous ignorance of this river could be desired, than that an untravelled gentleman, who had spent a great part of his life in the study of the geography of Africa, and knew everything written on the subject from the time of Ptolemy downwards, actually asserted in the 'Athenæum,' while I was coming up the Red Sea, that this magnificent river, the Leeambye, had "no connection with the Zambesi, but flowed under the Kalahari Desert, and became lost;" and "that, as all the old maps asserted, the Zambesi took its rise in the very hills to which we have now come." This modest assertion smacks exactly as if a native of Timbuctu should declare, that the "Thames" and the "Pool" were different rivers, he having seen neither the one nor the other. Leeambye and Zambesi mean the very same thing, viz. the RIVER.

Sekeletu intended to accompany me, but, one canoe only having come instead of the two he had ordered, he resigned it to me. After twenty minutes' sail from Kalai, we came in sight, for the first time, of the columns of vapour, appropriately called "smoke," rising at a distance of five or six miles, exactly as when large tracts of grass are burned in Africa. Five columns now arose, and bending in the direction of the wind, they seemed placed against a low ridge covered with trees; the tops of the columns at this distance appeared to mingle with the clouds. They were white below, and higher up became dark, so as to simulate smoke very closely. The whole scene was extremely beautiful; the banks and islands dotted over the river and adorned with sylvan vegetation of great variety of colour and form. At the period of our visit several trees were spangled over with blossoms. Trees have each their own physiognomy. There, towering over all, stands the great burly baobab, each of whose enormous arms would form the trunk of a large tree, beside groups of graceful palms, which, with their feathery-shaped leaves depicted on the sky, lend their beauty to the scene. As a hieroglyphic they always mean "far from home," for one can never get over their foreign air in a picture or landscape. The silvery mohonono, which in the tropics is in form like the cedar of Lebanon, stands in pleasing contrast with the dark colour of the motsouri, whose cypress-form is dotted over at present with its pleasant scarlet fruit. Some trees resemble the great spreading oak, others assume the character of our own elms and chestnuts; but no one can imagine the beauty of the view from anything witnessed in England. It had never been seen before by European eyes; but scenes so lovely must have been gazed upon by angels in their flight. The only want felt, is that of mountains in the background. The falls are bounded on three sides by ridges 300 or 400 feet in height, which are covered with forest, with the red soil appearing among the trees. When about half a mile from the falls, I left the canoe by which we had come down thus far, and embarked in a lighter one, with men well acquainted with the rapids, who, by passing down the centre of the stream in the eddies and still places caused by many jutting rocks, brought me to an island situated in the middle of the river, and on the edge of the lip over which the water rolls. In coming hither, there was danger of being swept down by the streams which rushed along on each side of the island; but the river was now low, and we sailed where it is totally impossible to go when the water is high. But though we had reached the island, and were within a few yards of the spot, a view from which would solve the whole problem, I believe that no one could perceive where the vast body of water went; it seemed to lose itself in the earth, the opposite lip of the fissure into which it disappeared, being only 80 feet distant. At least I did not comprehend it until, creeping with awe to the verge, I peered down into a large rent which had been made from bank to bank of the broad Zambesi, and saw that a stream of a thousand yards broad, leaped down a hundred feet, and then became suddenly compressed into a space of fifteen or twenty yards. The entire falls are simply a crack made in a hard basaltic rock from the right to the left bank of the Zambesi, and then prolonged from the left bank away through thirty or forty miles of hills. If one imagines the Thames filled with low tree-covered hills immediately beyond the tunnel, extending as far as Gravesend; the bed of black basaltic rock instead of London mud; and a fissure made therein from one end of the tunnel to the other, down through the keystones of the arch, and prolonged from the left end of the tunnel through thirty miles of hills; the pathway being 100 feet down from the bed of the river instead of what it is, with the lips of the fissure from 80 to 100 feet apart; then fancy the Thames leaping bodily into the gulf; and forced there to change its direction, and flow from the right to the left bank; and then rush boiling and roaring through the hills,—he may have some idea of what takes place at this, the most wonderful sight I had witnessed in Africa. In looking down into the fissure on the right of the island, one sees nothing but a dense white cloud, which, at the time we visited the spot, had two bright rainbows on it. (The sun was on the meridian, and the declination about equal to the latitude of the place.) From this cloud rushed up a great jet of vapour exactly like steam, and it mounted 200 or 300 feet high; there condensing, it changed its hue to that of dark smoke, and came back in a constant shower, which soon wetted us to the skin. This shower falls chiefly on the opposite side of the fissure, and a few yards back from the lip, there stands a straight hedge of evergreen trees, whose leaves are always wet. From their roots a number of little rills run back into the gulf; but as they flow down the steep wall there, the column of vapour, in its ascent, licks them up clean off the rock, and away they mount again. They are constantly running down, but never reach the bottom.

David Livingstone, MISSIONARY TRAVELS AND
RESEARCHES IN SOUTH AFRICA

*   *   *

The Union had liberated the universities from the dogmatic crudities and delimiting concepts of puritan theology and opened the fields of inquiry to native genius. Scotland is a country of extremes and the paradox was that many of the best scientists were ministers. Not so Clerk Maxwell, elected to the Chair at Marischal College at the age of 26:

In November 1856 he began work at Aberdeen. It is clear from his letters at this time that he devoted a great deal of thought and time to his classes and to the preparation of striking experiments for his lectures. He seems too to have kept a careful watch on his tongue, for in a letter to Lewis Campbell after he had been two months at Aberdeen he writes: "One thing I am thankful for

James Clerk Maxwell as a young man

though perhaps you will not believe it; up to the present time I have not even been tempted to mystify anyone", and again: "No jokes of any kind are understood here, I have not made one for two months and if I feel one coming I shall bite my tongue". His chief scientific work during the first two years at Aberdeen was his

Adams Prize Essay on "Saturn's Rings". This prize is awarded for the best solution of some problem of great scientific importance suggested by the electors. In this case the subject selected was the motion of Saturn's rings, and the point submitted was whether on one or any of the hypotheses (1) that the rings are solid, (2) that they are fluid or in part uniform, (3) that they consist of masses of matter not mutually coherent, the conditions of stability are satisfied by the mutual attractions and motions of the planet and the rings.

Maxwell came to the conclusion that the third hypothesis was the only one compatible with the stability of the rings. It was a very heavy and difficult investigation and took two years' hard work. It added greatly to his reputation and showed that a new star of the first magnitude had risen in the firmament of Mathematical Physics. Airy said of it that it was one of the most remarkable applications of mathematics he had ever seen.

The concluding paragraphs of the Treatise on Electricity and Magnetism:

"There appears to be in the minds of these eminent men some prejudice, or *à priori* objection, against the hypothesis of a medium in which the phenomena of radiation of light and heat, and the electric actions at a distance, take place. It is true that, at one time, those who speculated as to the causes of physical phenomena were in the habit of accounting for each kind of action at a distance by means of a special ætherial fluid, whose function and property it was to produce these actions. They filled all space three and four times over with æthers of different kinds, the properties of which were invented merely to 'save appearances,' so that more rational enquirers were willing rather to accept not only Newton's definite law of attraction at a distance, but even the dogma of Cotes [Preface to Newton's *Principia*, 2nd edition], that action at a distance is one of the primary properties of matter, and that no explanation can be more intelligible than this fact. Hence

128

the undulatory theory of light has met with much opposition, directed not against its failure to explain the phenomena, but against its assumption of the existence of a medium in which light is propagated.

"We have seen that the mathematical expression for electro-dynamic action led, in the mind of Gauss, to the conviction that a theory of the propagation of electric action in time would be found to be the very key-stone of electro-dynamics. Now we are unable to conceive of propagation in time, except either as the flight of a material substance through space, or as the propagation of a condition of motion, or stress, in a medium already existing in space.

"In the theory of Neumann, the mathematical conception called potential, which we are unable to conceive as a material substance, is supposed to be projected from one particle to another in a manner which is quite independent of a medium, and which, as Neumann has himself pointed out, is extremely different from that of the propagation of light.

"In the theories of Riemann and Betti it would appear that the action is supposed to be propagated in a manner somewhat more similar to that of light.

"But in all of these theories the question naturally occurs:—If something is transmitted from one particle to another at a distance, what is its condition after it has left one particle and before it has reached the other? If this something is the potential energy of the two particles, as in Neumann's theory, how are we to conceive this energy as existing in a point of space, coinciding neither with the one particle nor with the other? In fact, whenever energy is transmitted from one body to another in time, there must be a medium or substance in which the energy exists after it leaves one body and before it reaches the other, for energy, as Torricelli [*Lezioni Accademiche* (Firenze, 1715), p. 25] remarked, 'is a quintessence of so subtle a nature that it cannot be contained in any vessel except the inmost substance of material things.' Hence all these theories lead to a conception of a medium in which

129

the propagation takes place, and if we admit this medium as an hypothesis, I think it ought to occupy a prominent place in our investigations, and that we ought to endeavour to construct a mental representation of all the details of its action, and this has been my constant aim in this treatise."

(In the same centenary tribute Einstein wrote:

If we leave aside the important *special* results which Maxwell contributed in the course of his life to particular domains of physics, and confine our attention to the modification that he produced in our conception of the nature of Physical Reality, we may say that, before Maxwell, Physical Reality, in so far as it was to represent the processes of nature, was thought of as consisting in material particles, whose variations consist only in movements governed by partial differential equations. Since Maxwell's time, Physical Reality has been thought of as represented by continuous fields, governed by partial differential equations, and not capable of any mechanical interpretation. This change in the conception of Reality is the most profound and the most fruitful that physics has experienced since the time of Newton.)

from JAMES CLERK MAXWELL, A COMMEMORATION
VOLUME

About the time of the meeting of the British Association in Belfast in 1874, Maxwell wrote some verses:

In Memory of Edward Wilson,
Who repented of what was in his mind to write after section.

RIGID BODY (sings).

Gin a body meet a body
    Flyin' through the air,
Gin a body hit a body,
    Will it fly? and where?

Ilka impact has its measure,
 Ne'er a ane hae I;
Yet a' the lads they measure me,
 Or, at least, they try.

Gin a body meet a body
 Altogether free,
How they travel afterwards
 We do not always see.

Ilka problem has its method
 By analytics high;
For me, I ken na ane o' them,
 But what the waur am I?

Glazebrook, JAMES CLERK MAXWELL AND MODERN
PHYSICS

* * *

It is now something of a fashion for artists in the smaller countries to move into other spheres. For instance, Ibsen moved into Italy and Germany to look back and write about the society of Norway. Joyce, more recently, travelled to Trieste, Zurich and Paris to write a novel about Dublin on a specific day. Thomas Carlyle was one of the first Scotsmen to establish himself in London, in Cheyne Row; indeed, he was called the Sage of Chelsea.

He had not been greatly encouraged by his countrymen, and found London more congenial for his work, with its reference libraries and admiring disciples. However, in November 1865 Carlyle, now an old man, was elected Rector of Edinburgh University. The following April he went up to Edinburgh to be installed. Jane did not accompany her husband; she was now very frail. Carlyle's works may not be greatly read now, but his moral grandeur is still an example:

131

Monday, April 2nd, was the day of the installation, an elaborate ceremonial in the Music Hall of the University. The auditorium was crowded with students and invited guests, every available place filled. The University officials and professors, in the traditional academic robes of their various degrees—black and gold, scarlet and white, deep purple—walked slowly to their places. The Principal of the University was Sir David Brewster, the same Dr. Brewster who, as Editor of the *Edinburgh Encyclopedia* forty-seven years before, had given Carlyle his first literary work.

Carlyle had with him a few sheets of paper on which were headings and notes for his address, but he made no use of them. He stood up to speak and after a few words, with an impatient movement of his shoulders, he shook off the crimson and black gown of office and went quietly on with his speech. The whole address was pitched low; it was not an oration, not a performance with calculated pauses and gestures; he spoke gently and with friendliness, but his words were profound and expressed the ideas and ideals by which he had tried to guide his life since he left Edinburgh at the same age as the young men now before him.

He spoke of the enthusiasm of youth and adjured his young hearers to hold fast to it. He spoke of diligence, frugality, patience and pious awe, he extolled the doctrine of *silence*. He spoke of the study of history and talked for a little of the great figures of England and Scotland in the past; he distinguished between learning and wisdom and told them that wisdom of the heart should be their highest aim. He said the way would be hard but bade them be of courage and he ended with a quotation from the Master whose early teaching had meant so much to him.

This is what he said:—

I will wind up with a small bit of verse that is from Goethe also, and has often gone through my mind. To me it has the tone of a modern psalm in it in some measure. It is sweet and clear—the clearest of sceptical men had not anything like so clear a mind as that man had, freer from cant and misdirected notion of any kind than any man in these ages has been. This is what the poet says. It is a kind of marching music of mankind—

"The Future hides in it
Gladness and sorrow:
We press still thorow;
Nought that abides in it
Daunting us—Onward!

"And solemn before us,
Veiled, the dark Portal,
Goal of all mortal:—
Stars silent rest o'er us—
With doubt and misgiving.

"But heard are the voices,
Heard are the Sages,
The worlds and the Ages:
'Choose well, your choice is
Brief, and yet endless.

"'Here eyes do regard you
In Eternity's stillness:
Here is all fullness,
Ye brave, to reward you:
Work, and despair not.'"

One last word. *Wir heissen euch hoffen*—We bid you be of hope. Adieu for this time.

Carlyle stayed in Scotland for some weeks after the installation. Every day he wrote to Goody. On 21 April Mrs Carlyle went out:

Mrs. Carlyle went for a drive in the Park; she had with her a little dog (not her own, but a friend's) and she let him out of the carriage for a run. Another carriage, which was passing at the moment, upset the dog which lay on its back in the roadway yelping. Almost before the brougham could stop, Mrs. Carlyle had got out and picked up the little animal, which turned out to be more frightened than hurt. Mrs. Carlyle spoke courteously to the owner of the other carriage and then, with the little dog inside again, continued her drive. But the agitation and commotion had been too great; she had just strength enough to take off her bonnet and loosen the combs in her hair; then her hands lay quiet in her lap, one above the other, and she was dead. The coachman, having driven twice round the Park without any sign from his mistress, stopped, looked in, and discovered what had happened. He took her to St. George's Hospital at Hyde Park Corner, and then that night she was brought back to Cheyne Row.

The end of an ideal marriage. A week after Jane's death Carlyle wrote:

Thursday last she was committed to her Father's grave, in the Abbey Kirk at Haddington, and now sleeps there, as was the covenant between us forty years ago or nearly so. Her death was swift (as had always been her prayer); swift, I am led to think, almost as lightning from the skies; and she passed away as in a blaze of splendour. Victory (late, but bright skies and complete to her) crowning her whole noble life and her. For her life from the time we met was and continued all mine; and she had fought and toiled for me valiantly at all moments up to that last, how loyally, lovingly and bravely, and through what sore paths and difficulties is now known only to God and one living mortal.

THOMAS CARLYLE—LETTERS TO HIS WIFE,
ed. Trudy Bliss

*   *   *

Like Kelvin, Bryce was a Scot though born in Belfast (H. A. L. Fisher suggests that Bryce is a corruption of Bruce). Centred in Glasgow, Bryce's connection was with Oxford, with Dicey and others. A lawyer, politician and historian, he had travelled the United States in the 1880s, and by intense inquiry of the inhabitants had by 1887 completed The American Commonwealth *(only one sixth from books). While waiting for it to be published in December 1888 he travelled in Egypt and India and wrote some letters home.*

To his Mother

Thebes.
Jan. 2nd.

We have just reached this famous city after a delightful sail up from Denderah, whose temples we saw this morning. They are late, of the times of the Ptolemies and the Roman Emperors; it is curious to come down to these very modern times, which one knows from Rome and other parts of Italy; and to realize that the Egyptian religion was still going on, and in external appearance much as it had gone on two thousand years earlier—and that all this strange mixture of mystic theosophy with a rather repulsive animal worship and apparently a good deal of practical sensuality, was in full life at the time of Christ's life and the first preaching of Christianity. In fact the Egyptian religion from about 70 B.C. diffused itself a good deal over the world. Ladies worshipped Serapis in Rome, and all sorts of nasty rites went on for a couple of centuries in Italy among people who had lost interest in their own old religion. Like most of the other cities, this city and its temples stood on the edge of the Desert. Strange that in Egypt you step out of your house into a wilderness of stone and sand, which stretches twelve hundred miles west to the Atlantic. The presence of this awful unexplored and unexplorable waste and silent land must have had a great effect on the mind of the people, even more than the melancholy Ocean has had on the Irish and the Hebridean Scotch.

135

To his Mother
In the Hooghly River.
Nov. 30th, 1888.
(Madras, Dec. 5th.)

After four rather over-filled days in Calcutta, I am on shipboard again, welcoming the prospect of three perfectly lazy days, which I use to write to you. It is no effort to do so, but a rest to one's own mind filled with impressions and reflections to pour out some of them, so far as definite, to you. I have been nearly four weeks in India, and seen a great deal of its surface, a good deal of its governing class, and a little of the educated natives.

The Civil Service slightly disappoints one. There is a high average of ability among the service men in the upper posts,—'tis these chiefly I have seen—but a good deal of uniformity, and a want of striking, even of marked individualities. They are intelligent, very hard working, with apparently a high sense of public duty and a desire to promote the welfare of the people of India. But they seem rather wanting in imagination and sympathy, less inspired by the extraordinary and unprecedented phenomena of the country than might have been expected, with little intellectual initiative; too conventionally English in their ways of life and thoughts to rise to the position. Since the unhappy so-called Ilbert Bill there has been a marked change in the attitude of Europeans to natives, especially in Bengal, and the natives complain bitterly that the civilians as well as the military and the planters, treat them with arrogance and make them feel their social inferiority as well as political subordination.

They are more out of the stream of the world's thought and movement than one was prepared to find. Europe seems very far away. Society is monotonous; it is in some places more military than civil, in some more civil than military; it has nowhere the variety and sense of intellectual activity which one feels in England. . . .

The ablest and most interesting person is the Viceroy. He very civilly telegraphed to me (when he knew I was leaving today) from his journey, that I should dine with him last night, and I did so, and had a very long and interesting talk with him, ranging over the whole field. The advanced natives are vexed with him for not having kept up Lord Ripon's pace, but he does not seem to me to have done badly for them; whereas that worthy man so forced the pace as to provoke bitterness and throw things back. Lady Dufferin was very pleasant; she had done much good by her efforts for Indian women. . . .

It is far harder to have just notions regarding the natives. In Calcutta they were prepared to make quite a fuss about me; a musical party was given in my honour—a newspaper with report thereof is sent herewith, and inside it a copy of the programme—they issued an elegant card inviting guests to meet the "Professor" (!) M. P. There were some Europeans and Armenians as well as natives, but little fusion, the middle wall of partition stands between. The music was strange and interesting, especially a Persian love ditty, said to be of Hafiz, chanted with wild contortions of face to a monotonous air and queer instruments. . . .

Next day I met by invitation about twenty leading natives and had a long talk with them on public affairs. They complained of the indifference of England to India, and wanted to know what they could do. One could only answer that they must try to supply information, exact facts and just views, to the English, of course even this will effect little in the sense they desire. They dwelt on the expense of the government, and the little influence they had, and two or three spoke very bitterly on the hauteur with which Anglo-Indians treat them; this is the real difficulty. I urged them strongly to have nothing to do with English parties; not to go to Liberals any more than to Tories in England; nor suffer Indian questions to get sucked into the party vortex; they did not relish this. There was plenty of talent among them, and an excellent gift of expression; but, of course, it was impossible for either side to speak frankly to the other; they couldn't tell me what they thought of us, nor I what profound weaknesses we discover in them. Lord

Dufferin said to me that he could not find among them all a single man with initiative, with the sort of character and courage which gives strength for practical statesmanship. This has been so for generations. However, they were friendly and complimentary, and we parted with many cordial expressions. These Bengal people are, especially the Hindoos, quicker, more apt and willing to learn, and altogether more plausible than the men of Upper India, much like the Greeks under the Roman Empire; but Upper India holds them cowards and the English hate their upsettingness. A fine old Jesuit whom I met said the English had made a great mistake in providing so much cheap university education; that there is thus created a huge, restless, discontented class, superficially brilliant, anxious for Government work, because there is none else for it, but wanting in the higher moral qualities. We are making atheists, too, for when they drop Hinduism they don't become Christians. The two young Oxford missionaries whom I saw, very fine fellows who live like ascetics, High Churchmen, of course, spoke better of the natives, and deplored the attitude of Anglo-Indians; they liked Hindus better than Mohammedans, but admitted that conversion was difficult with both. However, it seems Christians increase much faster than the population, and they are hopeful of the future. At present the most accessible are the aboriginal tribes, these might all, they said, be converted as soon as we had the men. They did not think that religion had any great effect upon moral conduct.

Besides the viceroy I dined with and saw several other leading officials, all very civil, and have a fair impression of Calcutta, which consists of three distinct cities—native, commercial, European residential. It is quite modern, with no sights except the Botanic and Zoologic Gardens and Museum. The best point is the vast open space called the Meidan, where people ride and drive, the latter after dark. Society didn't seem to me a bit interesting, but probably less frivolous than English fashionables. It is, of course, less purely military and civil than up country, for there are barristers and merchants not a few. The houses are large, cool,

138

airy, each in a large plot of ground, often with lawn tennis. Multitudes of servants, just like slaves in ancient Rome. One would soon get lazy and demoralized. I wonder our men retain so much energy. To be arrogant and overbearing is natural. Habits of expense soon grow; already I have become reckless of rupees, one can't live cheaply, tho' many things are cheap, one ceases to try.

Exotic as we are—more so than formerly because people in the services and commerce run oftener to Europe—our dominion seems fairly based. One doesn't see why, if frontier wars can be averted with Russia and France, we should not reign for another century. But long before then internal conditions will have greatly changed. Altho' Caste and Hinduism seem slightly shaken so far, they are being undermined, and may come down with a run before fifty years.

Rajputana,
Jan. 16th, 1889.

. . . I hope Mr. Gladstone and Liberals generally will hold their peace about Indian questions and the National Congress; these things look very different when one is out here and are not to be solved by European formulæ. The great use of all this to me is to enlarge one's ideas of history, a world so unlike ours, yet more like the average world of the past. One feels like writing something, not in the way of describing India or arguing Indian questions, which I am quite incompetent to do, but of setting out the *impression* of India and its place in history as compared with the West and the notions as to human nature it suggests. All these impressions will fade fast enough when one recrosses the sea—I wish I could have conveyed them duly to all before the salt brine has washed them out. The Hindu Sages had a meaning in forbidding the pious man to cross the great water.

H. A. L. Fisher, BIOGRAPHY OF VISCOUNT BRYCE

Robert Louis Stevenson was born in Edinburgh in 1850 and died in his house at Vailima in Samoa 44 years later of a cerebral haemorrhage. His writing until then was regarded with some sentimentality and dismissed as romantic, though with style. At the time of his death he was engaged on Weir of Hermiston, *and though unfinished it is undoubtedly his masterpiece, revealing new depths of insight and command of character.*

It chanced in the year 1813 that Archie strayed one day into the Judiciary Court. The macer made room for the son of the presiding judge. In the dock, the centre of men's eyes, there stood a whey-coloured, misbegotten caitiff, Duncan Jopp, on trial for his life. His story, as it was raked out before him in that public scene, was one of disgrace and vice and cowardice, the very nakedness of crime; and the creature heard and it seemed at times as though he understood—as if at times he forgot the horror of the place he stood in, and remembered the shame of what had brought him there. He kept his head bowed and his hands clutched upon the rail; his hair dropped in his eyes and at times he flung it back; and now he glanced about the audience in a sudden fellness of terror, and now looked in the face of his judge and gulped. There was pinned about his throat a piece of dingy flannel; and this it was perhaps that turned the scale in Archie's mind between disgust and pity. The creature stood in a vanishing point; yet a little while, and he was still a man, and had eyes and apprehension; yet a little longer, and with a last sordid piece of pageantry, he would cease to be. And here, in the meantime, with a trait of human nature that caught at the beholder's breath, he was tending a sore throat.

Over against him, my Lord Hermiston occupied the bench in the red robes of criminal jurisdiction, his face framed in the white wig. Honest all through, he did not affect the virtue of impartiality; this was no case for refinement; there was a man to be hanged, he would have said, and he was hanging him. Nor was

140

it possible to see his lordship, and acquit him of gusto in the task. It was plain he gloried in the exercise of his trained facilities, in the clear sight which pierced at once into the joint of fact, in the rude, unvarnished gibes with which he demolished every figment of defence. He took his ease and jested, unbending in that solemn place with some of the freedom of the tavern; and the rag of man with the flannel round his neck was hunted gallowsward with jeers.

Duncan had a mistress, scarce less forlorn and greatly older than himself, who came up, whimpering and curtseying, to add the weight of her betrayal. My lord gave her the oath in his most roaring voice, and added an intolerant warning.

"Mind what ye say now, Janet," said he. "I have an e'e upon ye, I'm ill to jest with."

Presently, after she was tremblingly embarked on her story, "And what made ye do this, ye auld runt?" the Court interposed. "Do ye mean to tell me ye was the panel's mistress?"

"If you please, ma loard," whined the female.

"Godsake! ye made a bonny couple," observed his lordship; and there was something so formidable and ferocious in his scorn that not even the galleries thought to laugh.

The summing up contained some jewels.

"These two peetiable creatures seem to have made up thegither, it's not for us to explain why."—"The panel, who (whatever else he may be) appears to be equally ill set-out in mind and boady."—"Neither the panel nor yet the old wife appears to have had so much common sense as even to tell a lie when it was necessary." And in the course of sentencing, my lord had this *obiter dictum*: "I have been the means, under God, of haanging a great number, but never just such a disjaskit rascal as yourself." The words were strong in themselves; the light and heat and detonation of their delivery, and the savage pleasure of the speaker in his task, made them tingle in the ears.

When all was over, Archie came forth again into a changed world. Had there been the least redeeming greatness in the crime, any obscurity, any dubiety, perhaps he might have understood. But the culprit stood, with his sore throat, in the sweat of his mortal agony, without defence or excuse: a thing to cover up with blushes: a being so much sunk beneath the zones of sympathy that pity might seem harmless. And the judge had pursued him with a monstrous, relishing gaiety, horrible to be conceived, a trait for nightmares. It is one thing to spear a tiger, another to crush a toad; there are æsthetics even of the slaughterhouse; and the loathsomeness of Duncan Jopp enveloped and infected the image of his judge.

Archie passed by his friends in the High Street with incoherent words and gestures. He saw Holyrood in a dream, remembrance of its romance awoke in him and faded; he had a vision of the old radiant stories, of Queen Mary and Prince Charlie, of the hooded stag, of the splendour and crime, the velvet and bright iron of the past; and dismissed them with a cry of pain. He lay and moaned in the Hunter's Bog, and the heavens were dark above him and the grass of the field an offence. "There is my father," he said. "I draw my life from him; the flesh upon my bones is his, the bread I am fed with is the wages of these horrors." He recalled his mother, and ground his forehead in the earth. He thought of flight, and where was he to flee to? of other lives, but was there any life worth living in this den of savage and jeering animals?

The interval before the execution was like a violent dream. He met his father; he would not look at him, he could not speak to him. It seemed there was no living creature but must have been swift to recognise that imminent animosity; but the hide of the Justice-Clerk remained impenetrable. Had my lord been talkative the truce could never have subsisted; but he was by fortune in one of his humours of sour silence; and under the very guns of his broadside, Archie nursed the enthusiasm of rebellion. It seemed to him, from the top of his nineteen years' experience, as if he were marked at birth to be the perpetrator of some signal action, to set back fallen Mercy, to overthrow the usurping devil that sat, horned and hoofed, on her throne. Seductive Jacobin figments, which he had often refuted at the Speculative, swam up in his mind and startled him as with voices: and he seemed to himself to walk accompanied by an almost tangible presence of new beliefs and duties.

On the named morning he was at the place of execution. He saw the fleering rabble, the flinching wretch produced. He looked on for a while at a certain parody of devotion, which seemed to strip the wretch of his last claim to manhood. Then followed the brutal instant of extinction, and the paltry dangling of the remains like a broken jumping-jack. He had been prepared for something terrible, not for this tragic meanness. He stood a moment silent, and then—"I denounce this God-defying murder," he shouted; and his father, if he must have disclaimed the sentiment, might have owned the stentorian voice with which it was uttered.

Frank Innes dragged him from the spot. The two handsome lads followed the same course of study and recreation, and felt a certain mutual attraction, founded mainly on good looks. It had never gone deep; Frank was by nature a thin, jeering creature, not truly susceptible whether of feeling or inspiring friendship; and the relation between the pair was altogether on the outside, a thing of common knowledge and the pleasantries that spring from a common acquaintance. The more credit to Frank that he was appalled by Archie's outburst, and at least conceived the design of keeping him in sight, and, if possible, in hand, for the day. But Archie, who had just defied—was it God or Satan?—would not listen to the word of a college companion.

"I will not go with you," he said. "I do not desire your company, sir; I would be alone."

"Here, Weir, man, don't be absurd," said Innes, keeping a tight hold upon his sleeve. "I will not let you go until I know what you mean to do with yourself; it's no use brandishing that staff." For indeed at that moment Archie had made a sudden—perhaps a warlike—movement. "This has been the most insane affair; you know it has. You know very well that I'm playing the good Samaritan. All I wish is to keep you quiet."

"If quietness is what you wish, Mr. Innes," said Archie, "and you will promise to leave me entirely to myself, I will tell you so much, that I am going to walk in the country and admire the beauties of nature."

"Honour bright?" asked Frank.

"I am not in the habit of lying, Mr. Innes," retorted Archie. "I have the honour of wishing you good-day."

"You won't forget the Spec.?" asked Innes.

"The Spec.?" said Archie. "O no, I won't forget the Spec."

And the one young man carried his tortured spirit forth of the city and all the day long, by one road and another, in an endless pilgrimage of misery; while the other hastened smilingly to spread the news of Weir's access of insanity, and to drum up for that night a full attendance at the Speculative, where further eccentric developments might certainly be looked for. I doubt if Innes had the least belief in his prediction; I think it flowed rather from a wish to make the story as good and the scandal as great as possible; not from any ill-will to Archie—from the mere pleasure of beholding interested faces. But for all that his words were prophetic. Archie did not forget the Spec.; he put in an appearance there at the due time, and, before the evening was over, had dealt a memorable shock to his companions. It chanced he was the president of the night. He sat in the same room where the Society still meets—only the portraits were not there: the men who afterwards sat for them were then but beginning their career. The same lustre of many tapers shed its light over the meeting; the same chair, perhaps, supported him that so many of us have sat in since. At times he seemed to forget the business of the evening, but even in these periods he sat with a great air of energy and determination. At times he meddled bitterly, and launched with defiance those fines which are the precious and rarely used artillery of the president. He little thought, as he did so, how he resembled his father, but his friends remarked upon it, chuckling. So far, in his high place above his fellow-students, he seemed set beyond the possibility of any scandal; but his mind was made up—he was determined to fulfil the sphere of his offence. He signed to Innes (whom he had just fined, and who just impeached his ruling) to succeed him in the chair, stepped down from the platform, and took his place by the chimney-piece, the shine of many wax tapers from above illuminating his pale face, the glow of the great red fire relieving from behind his slim figure. He had to propose, as an amendment to the next subject in the case-book, "Whether capital punishment be consistent with God's will or man's policy?"

A breath of embarrassment, of something like alarm, passed round the room, so daring did these words appear upon the lips of Hermiston's only son. But the amendment was not seconded; the previous question was promptly moved and unanimously voted, and the momentary scandal smuggled by. Innes triumphed in the fulfilment of his prophecy. He and Archie were now become the heroes of the night; but whereas every one crowded about Innes, when the meeting broke up, but one of all his companions came to speak to Archie.

"Weir, man! That was an extraordinary raid of yours!" observed this courageous member, taking him confidentially by the arm as they went out.

"I don't think it a raid," said Archie grimly. "More like a war. I saw that poor brute hanged this morning, and my gorge rises at it yet."

"Hut-tut," returned his companion, and, dropping his arm like something hot, he sought the less tense society of others.

Archie found himself alone. The last of the faithful—or was it only the boldest of the curious?—had fled. He watched the black huddle of his fellow-students draw off down and up the street, in whispering or boisterous gangs. And the isolation of the moment weighed upon him like an omen and an emblem of his destiny in life. Bred up in unbroken fear himself, among trembling servants, and in a house which (at the least ruffle in the master's voice) shuddered into silence, he saw himself on the brink of the red valley of war, and measured the danger and length of it with awe.

145

He made a detour in the glimmer and shadow of the streets, came into the back stable lane, and watched for a long while the light burn steady in the Judge's room. The longer he gazed upon that illuminated window-blind, the more blank became the picture of the man who sat behind it, endlessly turning over sheets of process, pausing to sip a glass of port, or rising and passing heavily about his book-lined walls to verify some reference. He could not combine the brutal judge and the industrious, dispassionate student; the connecting link escaped him; from such a dual nature, it was impossible he should predict behaviour; and he asked himself if he had done well to plunge into a business of which the end could not be foreseen? and presently after, with a sickening decline of confidence, if he had done loyally to strike his father? For he had struck him—defied him twice over and before a cloud of witnesses—struck him a public buffet before crowds. Who had called him to judge his father in these precarious and high questions? The office was usurped. It might have become a stranger; in a son—there was no blinking it—in a son, it was disloyal. And now, between these two natures so antipathetic, so hateful to each other, there was depending an unpardonable affront: and the providence of God alone might foresee the manner in which it would be resented by Lord Hermiston.

These misgivings tortured him all night and arose with him in the winter's morning; they followed him from class to class, they made him shrinkingly sensitive to every shade of manner in his companions, they sounded in his ears through the current voice of the professor; and he brought them home with him at night unabated and indeed increased. The cause of this increase lay in a chance encounter with the celebrated Dr. Gregory. Archie stood looking vaguely in the lighted window of a book-shop, trying to nerve himself for the approaching ordeal. My lord and he had met and parted in the morning as they had now done for long, with scarcely the ordinary civilities of life; and it was plain to the son that nothing had yet reached the father's ears. Indeed, when he recalled the awful countenance of my lord, a timid hope sprang up in him that perhaps there would be found no one bold enough to carry tales. If this were so, he asked himself, would he begin again? and he found no answer. It was at this moment that a hand was laid upon his arm, and a voice said in his ear, "My dear Mr. Archie, you had better come and see me."

He started, turned round, and found himself face to face with Dr. Gregory. "And why should I come to see you?" he asked, with the defiance of the miserable.

"Because you are looking exceeding ill," said the doctor, "and you very evidently want looking after, my young friend. Good folk are scarce, you know; and it is not every one that would be quite so much missed as yourself. It is not every one that Hermiston would miss."

And with a nod and a smile, the doctor passed on.

A moment after, Archie was in pursuit, and had in turn, but more roughly, seized him by the arm.

"What do you mean? What did you mean by saying that? What makes you think that Hermis—my father would have missed me?"

The doctor turned about and looked him all over with a clinical eye. A far more stupid man than Dr. Gregory might have guessed the truth; but ninety-nine out of a hundred, even if they had been equally inclined to kindness, would have blundered by some touch of charitable exaggeration. The doctor was better inspired. He knew the father well; in that white face of intelligence and suffering, he divined something of the son; and he told, without apology or adornment, the plain truth.

"When you had the measles, Mr. Archibald, you had them gey and ill; and I thought you were going to slip between my fingers," he said. "Well, your father was anxious. How did I know it? says you. Simply because I am a trained observer. The sign that I saw him make, ten thousand would have missed; and perhaps—*perhaps*, I say, because he's a hard man to judge of—but perhaps he never made another. A strange thing to consider! It was this. One day I came to him: 'Hermiston,' said I, 'there's a change.' He

147

never said a word, just glowered at me (if ye'll pardon the phrase) like a wild beast. 'A change for the better,' said I. And I distinctly heard him take his breath."

The doctor left no opportunity for anticlimax; nodding his cocked hat (a piece of antiquity to which he clung) and repeating "Distinctly" with raised eyebrows, he took his departure, and left Archie speechless in the street.

The anecdote might be called infinitely little, and yet its meaning for Archie was immense. "I did not know the old man had so much blood in him." He had never dreamed this sire of his, this aboriginal antique, this adamantine Adam, had even so much of a heart as to be moved in the least degree for another—and that other himself, who had insulted him! With the generosity of youth, Archie was instantly under arms upon the other side: had instantly created a new image of Lord Hermiston, that of a man who was all iron without and all sensibility within. The mind of the vile jester, the tongue that had pursued Duncan Jopp with unmanly insults, the unbeloved countenance that he had known and feared for so long, were all forgotten; and he hastened home, impatient to confess his misdeeds, impatient to throw himself on the mercy of this imaginary character.

He was not to be long without a rude awakening. It was in the gloaming when he drew near the doorstep of the lighted house, and was aware of the figure of his father approaching from the opposite side. Little daylight lingered; but on the door being opened, the strong yellow shine of the lamp gushed out upon the landing and shone full on Archie, as he stood, in the old-fashioned observance of respect, to yield precedence. The Judge came without haste, stepping stately and firm; his chin raised, his face illumined, his mouth set hard. There was never a wink of change in his expression; without looking to the right or left, he mounted the stair, passed close to Archie, and entered the house. Instinctively, the boy, upon his first coming, had made a movement to meet him; instinctively, he recoiled against the

148

railing, as the old man swept by him in a pomp of indignation. Words were needless; he knew all—perhaps more than all—and the hour of judgment was at hand.

It is possible that, in this sudden revulsion of hope, and before these symptoms of impending danger, Archie might have fled. But not even that was left to him. My lord, after hanging up his cloak and hat, turned round in the lighted entry, and made him an imperative and silent gesture with his thumb, and with the strange instinct of obedience, Archie followed him into the house.

All dinner-time there reigned over the Judge's table a palpable silence, and as soon as the solids were despatched he rose to his feet.

"M'Killop, tak' the wine into my room," said he; and then to his son: "Archie, you and me has to have a talk."

It was at this sickening moment that Archie's courage, for the first and last time, entirely deserted him. "I have an appointment," said he.

"It'll have to be broken, then," said Hermiston, and led the way into his study.

The lamp was shaded, the fire trimmed to a nicety, the table covered deep with orderly documents, the backs of law books made a frame upon all sides that was only broken by the window and the doors.

For a moment Hermiston warmed his hands at the fire, presenting his back to Archie; then suddenly disclosed on him the terrors of the Hanging Face.

"What's this I hear of ye?" he asked.

There was no answer possible to Archie.

"I'll have to tell ye, then," pursued Hermiston. "It seems ye've been skirling against the father that begot ye, and one of his Maijesty's Judges in this land; and that in the public street, and while an order of the Court was being executit. Forbye which, it would appear that ye've been airing your opeenions in a Coallege Debatin' Society"; he paused a moment: and then, with

149

extraordinary bitterness, added: "Ye damned eediot."

"I had meant to tell you," stammered Archie. "I see you are well informed."

"Muckle obleeged to ye," said his lordship, and took his usual seat. "And so you disapprove of Caapital Punishment?" he added.

"I am sorry, sir, I do," said Archie.

"I am sorry, too," said his lordship. "And now, if you please, we shall approach this business with a little more parteecularity. I hear that at the hanging of Duncan Jopp—and, man! ye had a fine client there—in the middle of all the riff-raff of the ceety, ye thought fit to cry out, 'This is a damned murder, and my gorge rises at the man that haangit him.'"

"No, sir, these were not my words," cried Archie.

"What were yer words, then?" asked the Judge.

"I believe I said, 'I denounce it as a murder?'" said the son. "I beg your pardon—a God-defying murder. I have no wish to conceal the truth," he added, and looked his father for a moment in the face.

"God, it would only need that of it next!" cried Hermiston. "There was nothing about your gorge rising, then?"

"That was afterwards, my lord, as I was leaving the Speculative. I said I had been to see the miserable creature hanged, and my gorge rose at it."

"Did ye, though?" said Hermiston. "And I suppose ye knew who haangit him?"

"I was present at the trial; I ought to tell you that, I ought to explain. I ask your pardon beforehand for any expression that may seem undutiful. The position in which I stand is wretched," said the unhappy hero, now fairly face to face with the business he had chosen. "I have been reading some of your cases. I was present while Jopp was tried. It was a hideous business. Father, it was a hideous thing! Grant he was vile, why should you hunt him with a vileness equal to his own? It was done with glee–that is the

150

word—you did it with glee; and I looked on, God help me! with horror."

"You're a young gentleman that doesna approve of Caapital Punishment," said Hermiston. "Weel, I'm an auld man that does. I was glad to get Jopp haangit, and what for would I pretend I wasna? You're all for honesty, it seems; you couldn't even steik your mouth on the public street. What for should I steik mines upon the bench, the King's officer, bearing the sword, a dreid to evil-doers, as I was from the beginning, and as I will be to the end! Mair than enough of it! Heedious! I never gave twa thoughts to heediousness, I have no call to be bonny. I'm a man that gets through with my day's business, and let that suffice."

The ring of sarcasm had died out of his voice as he went on; the plain words became invested with some of the dignity of the Justice-seat.

"It would be telling you if you could say as much," the speaker resumed. "But ye cannot. Ye've been reading some of my cases, ye say. But it was not for the law in them, it was to spy out your faither's nakedness, a fine employment in a son. You're splairging; you're running at lairge in life like a wild nowt. It's impossible you should think any longer of coming to the Bar. You're not fit for it; no splairger is. And another thing: son of mines or no son of mines, you have flung fylement in public on one of the Senators of the Coallege of Justice, and I would make it my business to see that ye were never admitted there yourself. There is a kind of a decency to be observit. Then comes the next of it—what am I to do with ye next? Ye'll have to find some kind of a trade, for I'll never support ye in idleset. What do ye fancy ye'll be fit for? The pulpit? Na, they could never get diveenity into that bloackhead. Him that the law of man whammles is no likely to do muckle better by the law of God. What would ye make of hell? Wouldna your gorge rise at that? Na, there's no room for splairgers under the fower quarters of John Calvin. What else is there? Speak up. Have ye got nothing of your own?"

151

"Father, let me go to the Peninsula," said Archie. "That's all I'm fit for—to fight."

"All? quo' he!" returned the Judge. "And it would be enough too, if I thought it. But I'll never trust ye so near the French, you that's so Frenchifeed."

"You do me injustice there, sir," said Archie. "I am loyal; I will not boast; but any interest I may have ever felt in the French——"

"Have ye been so loyal to me?" interrupted his father.

There came no reply.

"I think not," continued Hermiston. "And I would send no man to be a servant to the King, God bless him! that has proved such a shauchling son to his own faither. You can splairge here on Edinburgh street, and where's the hairm? It doesna play buff on me! And if there were twenty thousand eediots like yourself, sorrow a Duncan Jopp would hang the fewer. But there's no splairging possible in a camp; and if you were to go to it, you would find out for yourself whether Lord Well'n'ton approves of caapital punishment or not. You a sodger!" he cried, with a sudden burst of scorn. "Ye auld wife, the sodjers would bray at ye like cuddies!"

As at the drawing of a curtain, Archie was aware of some illogicality in his position, and stood abashed. He had a strong impression, besides, of the essential valour of the old gentleman before him, how conveyed it would be hard to say.

"Well, have ye no other proposeetion?" said my lord again.

"You have taken this so calmly, sir, that I cannot but stand ashamed," began Archie.

'I'm nearer voamiting, though, than you would fancy," said my lord.

The blood rose to Archie's brow.

"I beg your pardon, I should have said that you had accepted my affront. . . . I admit it was an affront; I did not think to apologise, but I do, I ask your pardon; it will not be so again, I pass you my word of honour. . . . I should have said that I

152

admired your magnanimity with—this—offender," Archie concluded with a gulp.

"I have no other son, ye see," said Hermiston. "A bonny one I have gotten! But I must just do the best I can wi' him, and what am I to do? If ye had been younger, I would have wheepit ye for this rideeculous exhibeetion. The way it is, I have just to grin and bear. But one thing is to be clearly understood. As a faither, I must grin and bear it; but if I had been the Lord Advocate instead of the Lord Justice-Clerk, son or no son, Mr. Erchibald Weir would have been in a jyle the night."

Archie was now dominated. Lord Hermiston was coarse and cruel; and yet the son was aware of a bloomless nobility, an ungracious abnegation of the man's self in the man's office. At every word, this sense of the greatness of Lord Hermiston's spirit struck more home; and along with it that of his own impotence, who had struck—and perhaps basely struck—at his own father, and not reached so far as to have even nettled him.

"I place myself in your hands without reserve," he said.

"That's the first sensible word I've had of ye the night," said Hermiston. "I can tell ye, that would have been the end of it, the one way or the other; but it's better ye should come there yourself, than what I would have had to hirstle ye. Weel, by my way of it—and my way is the best—there's just the one thing it's possible that ye might be with decency, and that's a laird. Ye'll be out of hairm's way at the least of it. If ye have to rowt, ye can rowt amang the kye; and the maist feck of the caapital punishment ye're like to come across'll be guddling trouts. Now, I'm for no idle lairdies; every man has to work, if it's only at peddling ballants; to work, or to be wheeped, or to be haangit. If I set ye down at Hermiston, I'll have to see you work that place the way it has never been workit yet; ye must ken about the sheep like a herd; ye must be my grieve there, and I'll see that I gain by ye. Is that understood?"

"I will do my best," said Archie.

"Well, then I'll send Kirstie word the morn, and ye can go yourself the day after," said Hermiston. "And just try to be less of an eediot!" he concluded, with a freezing smile, and turned immediately to the papers on his desk.

R. L. Stevenson, WEIR OF HERMISTON

*　　*　　*

In the year 1896 there was an event to be noted. William Thomson, Lord Kelvin, had served the University of Glasgow for fifty years. The Jubilee was the occasion of an address presented to Lord Kelvin.

'The fifty years during which you have occupied the Chair of Natural Philosophy in this University have to an extent unparalleled in the history of the world been marked by brilliant discoveries in every department of Physical Science, and by the prompt adaptation of many of these discoveries to meet the practical needs of mankind. We recognise with admiration that in both these respects you have been a leader of the age in which we live. Your mathematical and experimental genius has unveiled the secrets of nature; your marvellous gift of utilising such discoveries has ministered in many ways to the happiness and dignity of human life. Your name and your work have been an inspiration to the physicists of the world: new departments of technical industry have sprung into existence under your hand; and even the unlettered have learned to value the gifts which science bestows. The justice of the tributes which have been paid to you by Universities and Scientific Societies at home and abroad, and by the Governments of this and other lands, we are proud to acknowledge. But only your colleagues in University work are in a position to appreciate the versatility of faculty, the exhaustless energy, and the tenacity of purpose which have enabled you to grapple successfully with problems the most varied, and to reveal to us on every side the reign of order and law. In the midst of all, you have endeared yourself to us by the graces of your personal character, notably by that simplicity which, unmarred by honours or success, remains the permanent possession of transcendent genius, and by that humility of spirit which, the clearer the vision of truth becomes, bows with the lowlier reverence before the mystery of the universe.'

Agnes Gardner King, KELVIN THE MAN

He was to live into the new century. He died on 17 December 1907. On 23 December before the great of the nation he was buried in Westminster Abbey by the side of Sir Isaac Newton.

*   *   *

Mary Slessor was born in Aberdeen in the middle of the nineteenth century into a home that was that mixture of godliness and filth, of piety and crudity that is a familiar texture of the tenements of Scottish towns. The conditions were a challenge to effort, and in the year after Livingstone's death she felt equipped to volunteer to serve in Calabar, fifty miles up from the Guinea coast. She was twenty-eight, and with occasional visits home, served there until her death in 1915.

"Don't grow up a nervous old maid! Gird yourself for the battle outside somewhere, and keep your heart young. Give up your whole being to create music everywhere, in the light places and in the dark places, and your life will make melody. I'm the witness to the perfect joy and satisfaction of a single life—with a tail of

Mary Slessor

human tag-rag hanging on. It is rare! It is as exhilarating as an aeroplane or dirigible or whatever that they are always trying to get up and are always coming down. God has been good to me, letting me serve Him in this humble way. I cannot thank Him enough for the honour He conferred upon me when He sent me to the Dark Continent."

Mary Slessor

Her Bible was her most earnest study. She read carefully, underlining significant words as she went along, writing her comments in margins. When one Bible was finished, she started another.

'Why do you do that?' she was asked. 'You have studied the Bible many times. Why continue to write in it?'

'My mind and thoughts can change over the years,' she defended herself.

When confronted with a difficult problem, she searched the Bible for advice. Some of her Bibles are still in existence, her comments clear in the narrow margins:

God is never behind time.
A gracious woman has gracious friendships.
Nature is under fixed and fine laws, but it cannot meet the need of man.
Good is good, but it is not enough; it must be God.
The secret of all failure is disobedience.
Unspiritual man cannot stand success.
Sin is loss for time and eternity.
An arm of flesh never brings power.
Half the world's sorrow comes from the unwisdom of parents.
Obedience brings health.
Blessed the man and woman who is able to serve cheerfully in the second rank—a big test.
Slavery never pays. The slave is spoiled as a man and the master not less so.

Brian O'Brien, SHE HAD A MAGIC

*   *   *

Scottish philosophy begins with Duns Scotus; and he emphasises one strain which is continually repeated with slight variations through European philosophy, as in Pascal. In his suggestion that the idea of individuation lies outside form and matter, he implies a notion of personality which can act in freedom and exercise choice. Theologically, when he proposes that the Incarnation is independent of the Fall he is asserting the uniqueness of the relationship to Christ as the prime source of self-knowledge for the Christian. It is the intensity of this experience that is shared by thinkers like Pascal and Kierkegaard.

H. R. Mackintosh of Edinburgh University gave an extensive review of Kierkegaard's work in his Croall lectures in the autumn of 1933:

Two assumptions, important for Kierkegaard's general point of view, are to be noted here. First, the principle of spiritual inwardness, or, as it is often called, subjectivity, has a determinative influence on all his thinking. By inwardness is meant the personal appropriation of Divinely presented truth, its apprehension with or through *passion*. As Brunner puts it, interpreting Kierkegaard with true insight:

Faith is a *suffering* . . . a shaking of the whole existence which can be compared only to what we call passion. In fact, it is a curiously mixed passion or suffering; it is even, as the classical Christian expression puts it, a death, the death of the old self, the autonomous Ego. And at the same time it is a joy; it is the resurrection of a new Ego.

Truth, Kierkegaard declares, is subjectivity, as subjectivity is truth. This, however, is by no means equivalent to the denial of given or objectively encountered reality, for it is on the objective that the soul feeds. His point rather is that the coldly objective counts for nothing by itself; or, as he expresses it in familiar words, 'only the truth that edifies is truth for thee.' Religious insight, that is to say, is higher and more veracious in proportion as it includes and, as it were, glows with that 'infinite passion' through which alone our right relation to God comes into being. There is no such thing as spiritual truth not fused with personal experience that costs. At every point the one question worth

158

asking is, 'What does this truth signify for my tragically real existence?' Knowledge of God's truth becomes ours only in the act of deciding for it with all our strength. Decision is no mere consequence of recognizing truth, it is a living and essential factor in apprehending it. To think subjectively—and no other kind of thinking matters here—is to act upon a risk. Cool detachment is an atmosphere in which we cannot believe, as the New Testament accounts believing. 'Thou art the man' are words which must sound in our ears perpetually if, in Kierkegaard's special phrase, our thought is to be 'existential'—i.e., carried on with the unfailing consciousness that we stand before God, guilty and blind, awaiting His judgment and mercy.

A mind so gravely realistic could never have been touched or tempted by the subjectivity of 'religion without an object'. On the other hand, two prominent forms of so-called objective thinking in religion awakened his bitter and scornful censure. One is the cold and futile objectiveness of speculative divinity, which dissolves the Gospel in ideas, rejects the unique incarnation of God in Christ, robs men thus of a commanding spiritual authority, and shirks the imperative duty of calling upon them to make up their minds for God. This is the unpardonable sin of thinking dispassionately about God and eternity. The other is the tepid objectiveness of conventional Churchmanship, which lives at peace with the world, atrophies the sense for spiritual heroism, and displaces personal concern about salvation by decent or prosperous membership of an institution. When Kierkegaard said that truth is subjectivity, then, he bade men recollect that personal Christianity without *decision* is nothing better than a phrase. We are set, each of us, in the inescapable presence of God; and to live and think as if it were not so is in fact not to think or live at all.

The second underlying principle for Kierkegaard is the rooted distrust of Hegelian philosophy in which, after years of storm and stress, he had ended. He now rested in an immovable conviction that Hegelianism, with its serene objectivity and optimistic acceptance of the actual, is the worst possible framework in which authentic Christian belief can be set. Hegel stood for the royal autocracy of human thought, the exclusive supremacy of the so-called creative reason of man; but to Kierkegaard nothing could be more falsely and sentimentally out of touch with the sombre facts of life as lit up by the flash of revelation. Here are all the materials for a great controversy; and the balance of forces in the fight changed when Kierkegaard stepped into the arena. 'The beginning of the new apprehension of the problem of God,' writes Karl Heim, 'dates from that moment in the nineteenth century when Kierkegaard, in conflict with the Hegelian philosophy, rediscovered the way back from abstract thought to the actually existing reality.' Hegel stood for the world as a closed system; his antagonist pointed to grim factors in life and thought which are incalculable. Hegel, with a higher naturalism, dissolved the individual in 'bloodless categories'; the other proclaimed the sheer individuality of conscience as it listens to God. Hegel found it possible to approve of Christianity as at all events a first sketch of the all-inclusive metaphysic; the other announced the paradox of God's self-revelation, by its nature an offence to reason, and only to be grasped through the infinite passion of faith.

Such a philosophy as Hegel's, it follows, is inwardly and unavoidably at odds with Christian religion; it will pass the wit of man to bridge the gulf. The Gospel asks of each man the question: Wilt thou be made whole? But philosophical idealism, taking its own characteristically frivolous view of sin, recoils with distaste from a query so intrusive: for its chief purpose is not to cleanse or cure, but to explain. In Kierkegaard's concise words:

Speculation can have nothing to do with sin; in fact, it ought not to have anything to do with sin. Sin belongs to the sphere of ethics; but ethical and speculative thought are moving in opposite directions. The latter abstracts from reality, the former makes for it. Hence it is that ethics operate with a category which speculation ignores and despises—viz., the individual.

H. R. Mackintosh, TYPES OF MODERN THEOLOGY

(*opposite*) Sir Alexander Fleming

*Professor Charles Pannett describes the situation of a Scottish
doctor working at St Mary's Hospital in London:*

"Here was Fleming, reticent, dour, acutely perceptive, more
aware than anybody that antiseptics were quite hopeless as
therapeutic applications. Yet he was the agent selected by
Providence to discover the most wonderful of all antiseptics and
at the same time open up a new field of investigation all over the
world.

"For the great discovery (of penicillin), Fleming was prepared in a very curious and interesting fashion. He was first afflicted with a cold, and being of an inquisitive disposition, he proceeded to culture some of his nasal secretion and found to his astonishment that it contained a substance inhibitory to bacterial growth and he traced this substance to his tears. Where they dropped on a culture plate clear spaces remained. He called the active substance lysozyme. Hitherto all known antiseptics had injured tissue cells more than bacteria. Here was one which was harmless to cells.

"The first stage in the discovery of penicillin had been accomplished.

"It was with a mind prepared in this way, and used to seeing hiatuses in bacterial cultures that he gazed upon that fateful Petri dish, contaminated with the unknown mould."

L. J. Ludovici, FLEMING: DISCOVERER OF PENICILLIN

The way to the discovery of penicillin was open.

*   *   *

As the centuries pass, they acquire a distinctive colour in the life of a nation. If we reckon those centuries since Copernicus, Galileo and Newton gave us a new view of the world, we could say that for Scotland the darkness of the seventeenth century gave way to the light and reason of the eighteenth. That in turn was followed by a century of great industrial and material expansion, but pre-eminently in the world of science Scotland's contribution to the store of knowledge was out of all proportion to the numbers of her people. History never repeats itself, and it may be that in the twentieth century the task of this people will be to give an example of compassionate living.

The Mosaic

In the eighth century before Christ Homer perceived that as a person follows a person he makes a line, but that a person can only penetrate and understand society as a mosaic.

In the twentieth century science has verified this. The discoveries of nuclear fission and DNA are the result of scientific activities scattered over the globe. There are knots, or as Solzhenitzyn might say, nodes, in the mosaic. An Einstein or Planck, a Crick or Watson, might temporarily give the illusion of finality, but it is the twentieth century's character that we are continually in motion like the universe, and we are constantly in relation, as star to star. And so a person in the twentieth century inheriting his unique gene and environment might after glancing at his line, look around him so that he might have an idea where he stands, always on the assumption that he will never truly or finally understand: and be convinced of this.

When I began acting in the late 'twenties, my life and ambitions were simple within the classical structure of the stage. One proceeded from extra to juvenile, to jeune premier (the French had a good name for it), to leading man, to heavy and so on. If one had a mind and the talent, one could ascend from Bernardo to Hamlet in one's lifetime. And indeed, in one's lifetime, if one had reached Hamlet by the time one was forty, one could go on playing it until one was seventy. Such was the repetitive structure of our society; and it was expected that if one's father was a doctor or a lawyer, one went into the firm, to carry on the line, to preserve continuity.

Two great wars, Darwin, Einstein and Freud have changed all this. In my own profession, radio, films and television (and such is the medium that it is with some heart-searching that I have omitted a reference to John Logie Baird) have altered my horizons so that I can no longer think of structures as vertical, to

163

be ascended by achievement and time. Life lies about us in a horizontal posture. And revelation is so complex that it does not lie within anyone's power (like Newton's) to reveal a comprehensive truth without reference to a parallel discovery. It is not merely literature or the expanding awareness of different civilisations that have imposed this change, but the necessity of life itself which suggests that our society must quite wilfully rise to a new level of openness in understanding differences. An Ibsen must understand a Chekhov, an Einstein, a Planck!

A Bedside Book can only suggest the environment in which this understanding happens. It can suggest something of the mosaic in the twentieth century, and the reader might perceive in the variety of life around him in Scotland something to pick to invite a moment of magic.

Hamewith

'En ma fin est mon commencement.'—Marie Stuart

Man at the end
Til the womb wends,
Fisher to sea,
Hunter to hill,
Miner the pit seeks,
Sodger the bield.

As bairn on breist
Seeks his first need
Makar his thocht prees,
Doer his deed,
Sanct his peace
And sinner remeid.

Man in dust is lain
And exile wins hame.

Sidney Goodsir Smith, from COLLECTED POEMS

Dr Bryce (author of The American Commonwealth) *invites some information and receives an autobiography in the form of a letter.*

From Dr Murray, Oxford
Residence: (Sunnyside, Banbury Road.)
15 Decr 1903

Dear Dr Bryce,

The less you say about *me* on Friday, the better pleased I shall be. I thought the occasion was to do honour to the birth place of the Dictionary, and to bring out the connexion of Mill Hill School with it, & that I should come in only incidentally, and when it could not be avoided. A subconscious fear that it might to some extent turn out otherwise, was one reason for my steady & repeated refusal to be present, ever since Dr McClure wrote to me about it in September. It was only last week that upon the persistent entreaties of the Old Millhillians, my own Old Boys, I consented to come; but it really *must not* be made an occasion of panegyrizing me, or dragging me into the foreground, and of thus giving scoffers occasion to say that you have reversed the role of Antony, and come not to bury Caesar, but to praise him. Better wait for the latter until you do come to bury me; then praise nor blame will disturb me. At present I feel it somewhat like getting me to attend my own obsequies, and I should really like to see the Dictionary finished first! I have lived & worked for it so long, that I should like to be able to say *Nunc dimittis*.

It is one of the hateful characteristics of a degenerate age, that the idle world will not let the worker alone, accept his offering of work, & appraise it for itself, but must insist upon turning *him* inside out, and knowing all about him, and really troubling itself a great deal more about his little peculiarities & personal pursuits, than his abiding work.

I should like to stop here and tell you nothing about myself. A 'voice crying in the wilderness' has always been for me a sort of

165

glorious ideal; and instead of raking up every scrap of useless detail about Chaucer & Shakspere, and Burns and Lamb, I often wish we knew nothing about any of them—especially of Burns & Lamb—but their splendid work.

Just to help you to orient yourself, however, and in the confidence that you—as a brother Scotsman—will not misuse it, I will try to give an outline answer to your inquiry into my philological history. I was *always* interested in language, especially in its *written* forms, since before I remember anything. I am reported to have known my letters before I was 18 months old, and when at that age a little brother was born to me, and I was introduced to him, it used to be told that I brought my primer—or *reading-made-easy*, and said 'I will show little brudder "round O" and "crooked S."' It was the greatest treat I could offer him. My mother who died at 80, a grand old Scotch woman, used to treasure up scraps of paper written in those days in which I had copied out words of Latin or Greek from books in which they occurred, & a Hebrew alphabet from the CXIX Psalm in a neighbour's big Bible. Of these I have only dim memories, but I have seen the scraps. I *do* remember a vigorous attack at the age of 7 upon a page of the Chinese Gospel of St. John, reproduced in the *Juvenile Missionary Magazine*, which I copied many times in very scrawly Chinese, and learned the characters for *Beginning, God, word, light, life, witness, man*, etc. by observing their recurrence in the columns, which I could write from memory many years after; indeed I fancy I could tell which is which still. Both my father & mother were of good family, but both families had come down in the world, and they were poor, and I had no chance of learning Latin till I was nearly 12, nor French for 2 years later. Greek, I learned mainly by myself two years later still. I was immensely indebted to Cassell's *Popular Educator* when it came out. After this, I had a sort of mania for learning languages; every new language was a new delight, no matter what it was Hebrew or Tongan, Russian or Caffre, I swallowed them all, at least so as to master grammar & structure, but rarely did enough at the vocabulary. Still I at one time or another could read in a sort of way 25 or more languages, at most of which I could still do something with the help of a dictionary. I was Junior Assistant Master in the Grammar School in Hawick for 3 years from the age of $17\frac{1}{2}$ to $20\frac{1}{2}$; then from 20 to 27 Master of the Subscription School called Hawick Academy. That was my great learning-time, when I made incursions into nearly all the sciences, botany, geology, entomology, anatomy, chemistry, mechanics, archaeology, electricity. I made Graham Bell, then a boy of 14, I a man of 24, his first electric battery, when I was attending his Father's Vacation Course in Vocal Physiology and Elocution in Edinr; he had confided to me his desire to know something about electricity, and we set about it in the old garden at Trinity near Edinr He calls me sportively 'the grandfather of the telephone'—a very remote ancestor, I tell him. At the age of 19 (!!) I was one of the founders of the Hawick Archaeological Society, which indeed I named, for the old men who were interested were going to call it the *Antiquarian* Society, when I demonstrated the superior potency of the word *Archaeological*, with such effect that they made me Secy. which I continued to be till I left Hawick in 1864. I am alas the only surviving member of its first years, and the Hawick people greatly want me to go to a Jubilee Celebration in 1906—so you must not bury me yet! In those days we were *men* at 19: I was earning my living, writing articles in the local paper, speaking at public meetings—always on the side of freedom and equality, and corresponding with learned archaeologists, geologists, & naturalists. To that time dates my friendship with Sir A. Geikie, his brother, & Dr Young of Glasgow, all then in the Survey—and a lesson on geology which I gave one day to Sir Roderick Murchison (without knowing who he was)—I took him for a simple tourist who was going to be imposed upon with a sham fossil, that a man wanted to sell him, and pointed out to him 'the utter absence of any organic structure.' How the Geikies did 'roar' when they heard of it! This was at 19; nowadays 'boys' at 19 are leaving school &

competing for scholarships, and preparing to begin life at 24. I taught from $17\frac{1}{2}$, & never cost my father a penny thenceforth.

About 1858, I think, the late Prince Lucien Bonaparte began to get versions of scriptural books done into local dialect; a Scotch St. Matthew was done by Henry Scott Riddell. A specimen of the Sermon on the Mount was reprinted in our local paper, and greatly disappointed me; it did not seem *living* Scotch at all. I tried my hand at doing better, had to invent a phonetic spelling for our Teviotdale sounds, abandoned Matthew, did half of Acts, & finally Ruth and Jonah—Ruth I published after as a specimen in my *Lowland Scotch* book. I planned & partly completed a phonetic key to Jamieson's Dicty. Then I noticed that Scottish grammar was not English, and I made a *Scotch Grammar*, showing that all the things that people called 'bad grammar' because they would be so in English, were 'good grammar' in Scotch. I read papers in these linguistic (& many other) subjects to the Archaeol. Soc. A stray copy of Bohn's Alfred the Great by Pauli with the Anglo-Saxon text of Orosius, picked up on a stall in Leith, opened a new world to me. I simply bathed & basked in it. Then at a meeting of the Berwicksh. Nat. Club at Alnwick, at which I represented our H^k society, I took part in a discussion of some local names, & showed some knowledge of Anglo-Saxon, on which Canon Greenwell came & introduced himself, asked where I had learned this. I told him and spoke of the difficulty of getting books. He sent me next day a large boxful from his own Library & that of the Chapter—there were Hooker and Lye & Thorpe & Thwaites, & the Heptateuch, & Durham Gospels—it was glorious! I made MS. copies of several whole books; I have them still & have often used them for the Dicty., to save a visit to Bodleian.

I wished to teach the world Anglo-Saxon. I prepared at the age of 20 a Grammar & First Reading-book, which I sent to the London publishers of Ahn's series & other language books known to me. They sent them back, & said such things would never pay; there was no demand for them; they were merely interesting to

168

half a dozen antiquarians. I have the MS. still. From one of the books Canon Greenwell sent me I learned Gothic—*Moeso-gothic* we called it then. I wanted the Gospels of Ulfilas greatly: James Douglas of Cavers (blessings on his memory) who had presented me with Raske's Anglo-Saxon Gram., now gave me a splendid copy of the text of the *Codex Argenteus*. I analysed every word in the Gospels, prepared a complete grammar & set of paradigms, which I never published; tho' when Prof. Skeat did one 10 or 15 years later, I could not help feeling how much better mine was! I worked on at Scotch in the light of Anglo-Saxon, & began to dream of sending my versions to Prince Lucien to see if he would print them.

In 1862 I was married; in 1863 my beloved & refined wife had a little daughter; she never recovered, fell into consumption, baby died, *she* died—a marriage, a birth, two deaths, all in 3 short years! To save her life, I had disposed of my school in Hawick, & came to the south of England, I could not afford to go farther, & I got a place in the Chartered Bank of India in Threadneedle Street. Doctors thought she might be saved with a milder winter; she survived the winter, but withered away with the summer, and I was left alone in London, doing uncongenial work, which yet I now see was useful for the Dictionary. Melville Bell had come to London & invented his 'Visible Speech,' he introduced me to A. J. Ellis, & took me to the Philological Society to hear his paper, told them I knew a lot about Scotch, & they asked me for a paper (which became the germ of my *Dialect of the Southern Counties of Scotland*). Then I learned of the existence of the Early English Text Society, & got hold of its edition of Hampole's Prick of Conscience in Northern Middle English. What a revelation! here in 14th c. Eng. of Yorkshire, I found my Southern Scotch in full bloom in an earlier form as a literary language, with its own grammar, precisely as I had made it out for Southern Scotch! This was in 1867. I rewrote my Scottish Grammar on historical principles, & thenceforth felt my interest more & more concentrated on English & its dialects. I did not lose my interest in

Russian or Hindustani or Achæmenian inscriptions, but I had not time for them, with all this new world of historical English. At the Phil. Soc. I met Dr Weymouth & criticized his papers. He asked who I was, learned that I was a bank clerk, had been a Schoolmaster, was an F.E.I.S. [Fellow of the Educational Institute of Scotland], & would probably be willing to return to scholastic work. He offered me a mastership at Mill Hill. I had married again, my present very able, wise, and helpful wife, a queen among women—we considered it & removed to Mill Hill, & were there 15 years, the central years of my life, and its Arcadian time. I went there a young man of 30, with 2 babies & left a middle-aged man of 45 with 9 children. I should never have left it but for the Dicty. I still look back to its rustic sweetness with tender longings.

There I took London Matric; 1st & 2nd BA. I was recommended to Black's to write the article English Language for the Encyclop. Brit., and prob. I knew the subject as well as anybody in 1873, better than most. Ednr gave me an LL.D.

A little later Harpers of N.Y. & Macmillans here wanted to get up a big dictionary to compete with Worcester & Webster. Somebody (I never knew who) told them I was the man to edit it. Macmillans sent for me & proposed it. I demurred, unless the dictionary was to be something vastly superior to any existing one; I could not waste my time nor interrupt my work at Mill Hill to make merely another Webster. They asked 'Had not the Philol. Soc. once contemplated making a Dictionary, & collected a quantity of materials? could not these be got? I knew nothing about the Phil. Society's scheme, which had died out some years before I joined the Society. But I inquired, got hold of some of the materials & with their aid prepared a specimen of what I thought a dictionary ought to be, which Macmillans put into type. Alas! its extent was far beyond their intentions, & still further beyond Harpers'. A whole year was spent in trying to contract my notions & expand theirs; but we never met. When it had reached the utmost minimum that I thought of any value, it was

170

still 50 per cent bigger than their utmost; so all came to an end.

But my specimen had been shown in the Phil. Soc. It showed what was possible. Everybody said if this could be done, how grand. 'Let us see if no publisher or body will look at it'. The specimen was shown to many, admired by many—the Cambridge Pitt Press very much regretted they had not money to tackle it. Finally Oxford looked at it with interest; had me here to see me & hear me explain it, got me to prepare fresh specimens of other words selected by them, to see that the *Carp-Casseage* specimen was a fair sample, had many discussions; & finally, after 2 years, said they would undertake the Dictionary, if I would edit it. Curiously enough I had never asked myself if I was prepared to do this. My interest in it was purely unselfish. I wanted to see an ideal Dictionary & show what I meant by one: *who* was to do it never crossed my mind. My own ideals were at the time all wrapped up in Mill Hill School; it was my little world; the time might come when I should be head of it, and I saw at once that the idea of my editing the Dictionary brought in serious considerations. I got a fortnight to decide; it was the most anxious fortnight my wife & I ever passed or ever may. We should have decided against it; but the dictionary would not be realized; when I hinted this decision to Bartholomew Price, he told me then that it would be all over with the Dictionary; the Delegates had understood all through, when I showed specimens, discussed points, & met objections, that I was willing to do it—they had seen me, heard me, knew me, believed that I could do it; they knew nothing about the Philological Society; they must have a responsible *man*; and if I 'drew back' & another man was looked for & found, the whole proceeding must begin anew, off at the ground, and 'believe me' he said 'it will never get as far as this again in our time'. This was then the alternative; I must sacrifice my dreams & hopes about Mill Hill, which had grown for 15 years, or the Dictionary ideal must fail. My wife bravely bade me choose the Dictionary; so did two of the Governors whom I consulted; Dr Weymouth also promised to do all he could to facilitate my position; and the Governors agreed to let me withdraw $\frac{1}{3}$ or even $\frac{1}{2}$ my time from the school, on condition of my sacrificing the same proportion of my salary. So I chose the Dictionary; but it was, I felt, a great sacrifice. As events turned out, it was a greater one than I thought: I dreamed of 10 years hard work; it has proved a life time's. And half of my time was not enough: the Dictionary demanded it all. In 5 years, I had to sever myself from M.H. entirely, & come to Oxford, giving the original Scriptorium erected in my garden at Sunnyside out in the village to the boys as a Reading Room; it was lifted up & placed in the Play ground, where I understand the Memorial building has been erected. This was in 1885; more than 18 years of incessant toil have followed. I have got able joint-Editors and Assistants, & we are still years from the end. I virtually bound myself to never ending toil, very different from the work of school with its recurrent holidays. I sometimes mourn, & chafe.

Yet I think it was God's will. In times of faith, I am sure of it. I look back & see that every step of my life has been as it were imposed upon me—not a thing of choice; and that the whole training of my life with its multifarious & irregular incursions into nearly every science & many arts, seems to have had the express purpose of fitting me to do this dictionary. I know philology & the history of the language intimately, and enough of nearly every other science & subject—chemistry, botany, entomology, archaeology, banking, commerce, stock exchange, to treat their terminology without help, or *to know when I do not know*, & need to ask help. I can at least write as a geologist to Prof. Geikie, as a botanist to Sir W. Thiselton Dyer, as an anatomist to Sir J. Burdon Sanderson, as a chemist to Roscoe or Thorpe, and not as the man in the street merely. And I know when an article I want to quote is wrong.

So I work on with a firm belief (at most times) that I am doing what God has fitted me for, & so made my duty; & a hope that He will strengthen me to see the end of it. He has been so good to me, & led me so wondrously, that I cannot but trust Him. But I am only an instrument, only the means that He has provided, & there is no credit due to me, except that of trying to do my duty; *Deo soli gloria*; and I wish from my heart that people would accept my work at the Dictionary as my simple effort to do my duty, and leave me quietly to do it, giving me wherewith to do it *well*, & without the pecuniary struggle that it has so often been, since I undertook it. Yet this too is no doubt also the divine plan for me, and will one day also be seen to have been all for the best.

J. A. H. Murray.

from SIR JAMES A. H. MURRAY

*   *   *

The mosaic is composed as man grows in understanding of what lies about him and changes it as his imagination is fired. As with the transforming of words in a foreign tongue into something familiar to him.

At a symposium in America in the 1950s, Edwin Muir gave his views on translation:

Translation is obviously a difficult art: I use that word, for if translation is not an art it can hardly be called translation. Yet it is a secondary art, and at best can strive for but never reach perfection. My own experience is mainly of translation from the German, and there, as a beginning, one must change the order of the words, and to do that with a great prose work is to commit an irremediable but unavoidable injury against it. I am thinking of Franz Kafka, whom my wife and I spent years in translating. The word order of Kafka is naked and infallible; it not only expresses his meaning but is involved as part of it; only in that order could he have said what he wanted to say. Yet the fine order has to be disarranged, the original edifice of the sentence dismantled and put up again. And the result can never be quite satisfactory, simply because the words run differently.

No other modern writer has made them run more easily and naturally than Kafka, so easily and naturally, indeed, that his style never strikes one as being acquired by study and practice, but simply to be there, like the intonation of a voice. So our main problem was to write an English prose as natural in the English way as his was in his own way.

Edwin Muir, from ON TRANSLATION,
ed. R. A. Brower

But the Scots are in almost a unique position as to translation. They have two languages, Scots and English: and it is really left to the discrimination of the poet as to the nature of the subject which to choose. Of the five translations here from Latin, French, German and Russian, a compiler might wish to say only two things: for many reasons Proust into Scots will not go; and Edwin Morgan's Scots seems to me to fit Mayakovsky's imagination beautifully.

Virgil into Scots

The Prologue to Book XIII

Heir begynnys the Proloug of the Threttene
and last Buk of Eneados ekit to Virgill
be Mapheus Vegius

Towart the evyn, amyd the symmyris heit,
Quhen in the Crab Appollo held hys sete,
Duryng the joyus moneth tyme of June,
As gone neir was the day and supper doyn,
I walkyt furth abowt the feildis tyte,

Quhilkis tho replenyst stud full of delyte,
With herbys, cornys, catal, and frute treis,
Plente of stoir, byrdis and byssy beys,
In amerant medis fleand est and west,
Eftir laubour to tak the nychtis rest.
And as I lukit on the lift me by,
All byrnand red gan walxin the evyn sky:
The son enfyrit haill, as to my sight,
Quhirlit about hys ball with bemys brycht,
Declynand fast towart the north in deid,
And fyry Phegon, his dun nychtis steid,
Dowkit hys hed sa deip in fludis gray
That Phebus rollis doun undir hell away;
And Esperus in the west with bemys brycht
Upspryngis, as forrydar of the nycht.

Gavin Douglas, from THE OXFORD BOOK OF
SCOTTISH VERSE

Rabelais into English

A Continuation of the Storm, with a short Discourse on the
Subject of making Testaments at Sea.

To make ones last Will, said *Epistemon*, at this time that we ought
to bestir our selves and help our Seamen, on the penalty of being
drown'd, seems to me as idle and ridiculous a Maggot as that of
some of *Cæsar*'s Men, who at their coming into the *Gauls*, were
mightily busi'd in making Wills and Codicils, bemoan'd their
Fortune, and the absence of their Spouses and Friends at *Rome*,
when it was absolutely necessary for them to run to their Arms,
and use their utmost Strength against *Ariovistus* their Enemy.

This also is to be as silly, as that jolt-headed Loblolly of a
Carter, who, having laid his Waggon fast in a Slough, down on his
Marrow-bones, was calling on the strong-Back'd Deity *Hercules*,
might and main, to help him at a dead lift, but all the while forgot

175

to goad on his Oxen, and lay his Shoulder to the Wheels, as it behoved him, as if a *Lord have mercy upon us* alone, would have got his Cart out of the Mire.

What will it signify to make your Will now? For either we shall come off, or drown for't. If we scape, it will not signifie a straw to us; for Testaments are of no value or Authority, but by the death of the Testators. If we are drown'd, will it not be drown'd too? Pr'ythee who will transmit it to the Executors? Some kind Wave will throw it ashoar, like *Ulysses*, reply'd *Panurge*, and some King's Daughter, going to fetch a Walk in the fresco on the Evening, will find it, and take care to have it prov'd and fulfill'd; nay, and have some stately *Cenotaph* erected to my Memory, as *Dido* had to that of her good Man *Sichæus*; *Æneas* to *Deiphobus* upon the *Trojan* shoar near *Rhœte*; *Andromache* to *Hector* in the City of *Buthrot*; *Aristotle* to *Hermias* and *Eubulus*; the *Athenians* to the Poet *Euripides*; the *Romans* to *Drusus* in *Germany*; and to *Alexander Severus* their Emperor in the *Gauls*; *Argentier* to *Callaischre*; *Xenocrates* to *Lisidices*; *Timares* to his Son *Teleutagoras*; *Eupolis* and *Aristodice* to their Son *Theotimus*; *Onestes* to *Timocles*; *Callimachus* to *Sopolis* the Son of *Dioclides*; *Catullus* to his Brother; *Statius* to his Father; *Germain* of *Brie* to *Hervé* the *Breton* Tarpawlin. Art thou mad, said Fryar *Jhon*, to run on at this rate? Help here, in the name of five hundred thousand millions of Cartloads of Devils, help; may a Shanker gnaw thy Moustachio's, and three rows of Pock-royals and Colly-flowers cover thy Bum and Turd-barrel instead of Breeches and Codpiece. Codsooks, our Ship is almost overset. Ods death, how shall we clear her? 'Tis well if she don't founder. What a Devilish Sea there runs? She'll neither try, nor hull, the Sea will overtake her, so we shall never scape, the Devil scape me. Then *Pantagruel* was heard to make a sad Exclamation, saying with a loud voice, Lord save us, we perish: Yet not as he would have it, but thy holy Will be done. The Lord and the blessed Virgin be with us said *Panurge*: Holos, alas, I drown, be be be bous, be bous bous: *In manus*. Good Heaven, send me some Dolphin to carry me safe on

shoar, like a pretty little *Arion*: I shall make shift to sound the
Harp if it be not unstrung. Let nineteen Legions of black Devils
seize me, said Fryar *Jhon*, (the Lord be with us, whisper'd
Panurge between his chattering Teeth) If I come down to thee, I'll
shew thee to some purpose, that the Badge of thy Humanity
dangles at a Calves Breech, thou ragged horn'd Cuckoldy Booby;
mgna, mgnan, mgnan: Come hither and help us thou great
weeping Calf, or may thirty millions of Devils leap on thee; wilt
thou come, Sea-Calf? Fye, how ugly the howling Whelp looks!
What, always the same Ditty? Come on now my bonny Drawer.
This he said, opening his Breviary, come forward, thou and I must
be somewhat serious for a while, let me peruse thee stiffly. *Beatus
vir qui non abiit*. Pshaw, I know all this by heart; let's see the
Legend of Monsieur St. *Nicholas*.

Horrida *Tempestas montem* turbavit *acutum*.

Tempest was a mighty Flogger of Lads at *Mountague College*.
If *Pendants* be damn'd for whipping poor little innocent wretches
their Scholars, he is, upon my Honour by this time fix'd within
Ixion's Wheel lashing the cropt ear bobtail'd Cur that gives it
motion. If they are sav'd for having whipp'd innocent Lads, he
ought to be above the——

Rabelais, GARGANTUA, translated by Sir Thomas
Urquhart of Cromarty and P. le Motteux

Heine into Scots

Lassie, What Mair Wad You Hae?

(Du hast Diamanten und Perlen)

O you're braw wi' your pearls and your diamonds,
  You've routh o' a' thing, you may say,
And there's nane has got bonnier een, Kate:
  'Od, lassie, what mair wad you hae?

177

I've written a hantle o' verses,
  That'll live till the Hendmost Day;
And they're a' in praise o' your een, Kate:
  'Od, lassie, what mair wad you hae?

Your een, sae blue and sae bonny,
  Have plagued me till I am fey,
'Deed, I hardly think I can live, Kate:
  'Od, lassie, what mair wad you hae?

Alexander Gray, from THE OXFORD BOOK OF
SCOTTISH VERSE

Proust into English

Introducing the men-women, descendants of those of the inhabitants of
Sodom who were spared by the fire from heaven.

*La femme aura Gomorrhe et l'homme aura
Sodome.* Alfred de Vigny.

The reader will remember that, long before going that day (on the
evening of which the Princesse de Guermantes was to give her
party) to pay the Duke and Duchess the visit which I have just
described, I had kept watch for their return and had made, in the
course of my vigil, a discovery which, albeit concerning M. de
Charlus in particular, was in itself so important that I have until
now, until the moment when I could give it the prominence and
treat it with the fulness that it demanded, postponed giving any
account of it. I had, as I have said, left the marvellous point of
vantage, so snugly contrived for me at the top of the house,
commanding the broken and irregular slopes leading up to the
Hôtel de Bréquigny, and gaily decorated in the Italian manner by
the rose-pink campanile of the Marquis de Frécourt's stables. I
had felt it to be more convenient, when I thought that the Duke
and Duchess were on the point of returning, to post myself on the
staircase. I regretted somewhat the abandonment of my watch-
tower. But at that time of day, namely the hour immediately
following luncheon, I had less cause for regret, for I should not

178

then have seen as in the morning, the footmen of the Bréquigny-Tresmes household, converted by distance into minute figures in a picture, make their leisurely ascent of the abrupt precipice, feather-brush in hand, behind the large, transparent flakes of mica which stood out so charmingly upon its ruddy bastions. Failing the geologist's field of contemplation, I had at least that of the botanist, and was peering through the shutters of the staircase window at the Duchess's little tree and at the precious plant, exposed in the courtyard with that insistence with which mothers "bring out" their marriageable offspring, and asking myself whether the unlikely insect would come, by a providential hazard, to visit the offered and neglected pistil. My curiosity emboldening me by degrees, I went down to the ground-floor window, which also stood open with its shutters ajar. I could hear distinctly, as he got ready to go out, Jupien who could not detect me behind my blind, where I stood perfectly still until the moment when I drew quickly aside in order not to be seen by M. de Charlus, who, on his way to call upon Mme. de Villeparisis, was slowly crossing the courtyard, a pursy figure, aged by the strong light, his hair visibly grey. Nothing short of an indisposition of Mme. de Villparisis (consequent on the illness of the Marquis de Fierbois, with whom he personally was at daggers drawn) could have made M. de Charlus pay a call, perhaps for the first time in his life, at that hour of the day. For with that eccentricity of the Guermantes, who, instead of conforming to the ways of society, used to modify them to suit their own personal habits (habits not, they thought, social, and deserving in consequence the abasement before them of that thing of no value, Society—thus it was that Mme. de Marsantes had no regular "day," but was at home to her friends every morning between ten o'clock and noon), the Baron, reserving those hours for reading, hunting for old curiosities and so forth, paid calls only between four and six in the afternoon. At six o'clock he went to the Jockey Club, or took a stroll in the Bois. A moment later, I again recoiled, in order not to be seen by Jupien. It was nearly time for him to start for the office, from which he would return only for dinner, and not even then always during the last week, his niece and her apprentices having gone to the country to finish a dress there for a customer. Then, realising that no one could see me, I decided not to let myself be disturbed again, for fear of missing, should the miracle be fated to occur, the arrival, almost beyond the possibility of hope (across so many obstacles of distance, of adverse risks, of dangers), of the insect sent from so far as ambassador to the virgin who had so long been waiting for him to appear. I knew that this expectancy was no more passive than in the male flower, whose stamens had spontaneously curved so that the insect might more easily receive their offering; similarly the female flower that stood here, if the insect came, would coquettishly arch her styles, and, to be more effectively penetrated by him, would imperceptibly advance, like a hypocritical but ardent damsel, to meet him half-way. The laws of the vegetable kingdom are themselves governed by other laws, increasingly exalted. If the visit of an insect, that is to say, the transportation of the seed of one flower is generally necessary for the fertilisation of another, that is because autofecundation, the fertilisation of a flower by itself, would lead, like a succession of intermarriages in the same family, to degeneracy and sterility, whereas the crossing effected by the insects gives to the subsequent generations of the same species a vigour unknown to their forebears. This invigoration may, however, prove excessive, the species develop out of all proportion; then, as an anti-toxin protects us against disease, as the thyroid gland regulates our adiposity, as defeat comes to punish pride, fatigue indulgence, and as sleep in turn depends upon fatigue, so an exceptional act of autofecundation comes at a given point to apply its turn of the screw, its pull on the curb, brings back within normal limits the flower that has exaggerated its transgression of them. My reflexions had followed a tendency which I shall describe in due course, and I had already drawn from the visible stratagems of flowers a conclusion that bore upon a whole unconscious element of literary work, when I saw M. de Charlus coming away from the

Marquise. Perhaps he had learned from his elderly relative herself, or merely from a servant, the great improvement, or rather her complete recovery from what had been nothing more than a slight indisposition. At this moment, when he did not suspect that anyone was watching him, his eyelids lowered as a screen against the sun, M. de Charlus had relaxed that tension in his face, deadened that artificial vitality, which the animation of his talk and the force of his will kept in evidence there as a rule. Pale as marble, his nose stood out firmly, his fine features no longer received from an expression deliberately assumed a different meaning which altered the beauty of their modelling; nothing more now than a Guermantes, he seemed already carved in stone, he Palamède the Fifteenth, in their chapel at Combray. These general features of a whole family took on, however, in the face of M. de Charlus a fineness more spiritualised, above all more gentle. I regretted for his sake that he should habitually adulterate with so many acts of violence, offensive oddities, tale-bearings, with such harshness, susceptibility and arrogance, that he should conceal beneath a false brutality the amenity, the kindness which, at the moment of his emerging from Mme. de Villeparisis's, I could see displayed so innocently upon his face. Blinking his eyes in the sunlight, he seemed almost to be smiling, I found in his face seen thus in repose and, so to speak, in its natural state something so affectionate, so disarmed, that I could not help thinking how angry M. de Charlus would have been could he have known that he was being watched; for what was suggested to me by the sight of this man who was so insistent, who prided himself so upon his virility, to whom all other men seemed odiously effeminate, what he made me suddenly think of, so far had he momentarily assumed her features, expression, smile, was a woman.

M. Proust, REMEMBRANCE OF THINGS PAST—CITIES OF THE PLAIN, translated by C. K. Scott-Moncrieff

Mayakovsky into Scots

Anent the Deeference o Tastes

A cuddy,
      goavin at a camel,
            lauchit:
"Whit
    kinna cuddy's yon,
            aa bim-bam-bauchlt?"
The camel skrieked:
         "Ye caa yirsel a cuddy?
Ye're naethin
      but a scrunty
         shilpit camel!"
—Ach,
    lat auld Frosty-Pow abune unscrammle
the twa puir craturs:
          he
           kens the brose fae the gundy.
              1929

Edwin Morgan, WI' THE HAILL VOICE

*   *   *

A rebel's description of socialism:

It was as a school-teacher that Maxton gained his first clear insight into the impoverished lives of the workers and their children. At the Martyrs' School in Townhead he saw not merely a monument to martyrs for religious faith but the living martyrdom of the little derelicts of Glasgow's industrialism. He saw little children come hungry to school. He saw them come ragged and bootless on cold winter mornings. He asked, "Why?" He kept on asking, "Why?"

He quickly indicted the Capitalist system with the responsibility, and accepted Socialism as the only alternative. He saw the Socialist Commonwealth in simple terms of the better distribution of the ordinary commodities and necessities of life.

"Socialism," he said years later, when presenting certificates to foundation members of the I.L.P., "means nothing to me, if it does not mean that as I have a house to live in, you also have a house to live in; that as I have food to eat, you also have food to eat; that as I have education, recreation and leisure, you also have education, recreation and leisure."

Gilbert McAlister, JAMES MAXTON: THE PORTRAIT OF
A REBEL

*   *   *

John Grierson was born in 1898 in a village near Stirling. His father was a dominie, his grandfather a lighthouse-keeper. During World War I he served on minesweepers: after that he took an MA degree at Glasgow University, with distinctions in English and Moral Philosophy. He decided to make his career in films. In doing so he coined a word:

I grew up in the Clydeside movement. I've been in politics all my life. Nobody who ever grew up in the Clydeside movement forgets. Under no circumstances do we forget. But whether I went into politics in the ordinary sense was another matter . . . No, I thought I'd do a better political job the way I did, and I was very interested in this question of putting the working class on the screen, of bringing the working class thing alive in another form than we were getting on the soapboxes of Glasgow Green . . . Now, if you think of the cinema, the motion picture, round about the twenties, you have a tradition of its being used for theatrical purposes and developing quite a big tradition in comedy and also

183

in theatrical shapes, through people like DeMille and D W Griffith and so on . . . There were newsreels. These were very superficial accounts of pageants, fires, disasters, parades, national celebrations, army celebrations, things of that kind.. . . There was a whole world undiscovered, a whole area of cinematic possibility undiscovered. All we did in documentary was we occupied Oklahoma. I saw this thing. I saw here was a territory completely unoccupied . . . The only thing was to find a way of financing it. And, of course, the great event in the history of documentary was that we didn't go to Hollywood for money. We went to governments for money and thereby tied documentary, the use of the realistic cinema, to purposes . . .

I suppose I coined the word (documentary) in the sense that I wasn't aware of its being used by anybody else. I mean, to talk about a documentary film was new, and I know I was surprised when I went over to Paris in 1927 and found them talking about '*filmes documentaires*'. Now, I must have seen that before, but I wasn't aware of it. When I used the word 'documentary' of Bob Flaherty's *Moana*, I was merely using it as an adjective. Then I got to using it as a noun: 'the documentary'; 'this is documentary'. The word 'documentary' became associated with my talking about this kind of film, and with me and a lot of people round me. There was a period (I think you'll find some very curiously mixed evidence on this subject) when some of them tried to get rid of the 'documentary' because it was felt to be very ugly. And Caroline Lejeune in *The Observer* kept saying, "Why the devil do we hang on to this gruesome word 'documentary'?" I said at the time, "Well, I think we'd better hang on to this word because if it's so ugly, nobody will steal it." And that, of course, is what happened. It was so ugly that nobody would steal it.

Elizabeth Sussex, an interview with Grierson in THE
RISE AND FALL OF BRITISH DOCUMENTARY

*   *   *

Daily Record Buildings,
Glasgow, designed by
Charles Rennie Mackintosh

185

A curator and his place—from an introduction to an exhibition of Glasgow University's pictures at Colnaghi's.

The University of Glasgow is nearly five-and-a-quarter centuries old. It was founded in 1451 by Pope Nicholas V, who endowed it with the privileges of the University of Bologna. Among British universities it comes, in order of antiquity, after only Oxford, Cambridge, and St Andrews; it is over 100 years older than Edinburgh and something between 350 and 400 years older than any of the English civic universities.

It would be extravagant to claim that all these many years of history have been equally distinguished. During its first century the University's very existence was at times precarious; and, for most of the next 200 years, it was still small and modest. In the eighteenth century, however, it blossomed. As the university that produced and nurtured Adam Smith and in which *The Wealth of Nations* was written, it became a recognized European centre of learning. It was also in the eighteenth century that interest in the visual arts—fostered by Adam Smith's teacher and predecessor in the chair of Moral Philosophy, the aesthetician Francis Hutcheson—led to them attaining a kind of academic status.

In 1753 the brothers, Robert and Andrew Foulis, who had begun as the University's printers, established in one of the College's largest rooms an academy for the training of painters, sculptors, and engravers—a venture which, as Glasgow is always ready to remind London, pre-dates the founding of the Royal Academy by fifteen years. As samples of the highest excellence Robert, an ardent if somewhat gullible collector, accumulated some 450 pictures including thirty-eight which he believed to be by Raphael, twenty-one by Titian, thirty-five by Rubens, eight by Rembrandt, and others, in smaller quantities, labelled as Leonardo, Michelangelo, Correggio, Andrea del Sarto, Veronese, Tintoretto, Poussin, Claude, Van Dyck, and Bruegel. The venture, with a catalogue that read like a dictionary of artists,

186

was, of course, absurdly over-ambitious. After Robert Foulis's death and the Academy's demise in 1776, the collection was sold at Christie's where, even in an age when grandiose attributions were more acceptable than they are today, it realized a paltry £398 5*s*.

It is easy to treat the whole Foulis story as a kind of comedy—a comedy, albeit, with its tragic side. This would, however, be an underestimate of what the brothers did, as distinct from their way of doing it. Their achievement, born in a spirit of enterprise comparatively rare in academic communities, was to take action that was both enthusiastic and bold. Despite their mistakes they generated a consciousness of art which had a continuing presence in Glasgow, and among Glaswegians who had moved to other places. The befriender of the Academy's students when they made their *de rigueur* visits to Rome was the Glasgow alumnus, Gavin Hamilton, that learned connoisseur, antiquary, and painter of Neoclassical pictures; and, from a later generation, William Buchanan, the most spectacular art dealer of the early nineteenth century, had been a student at a time when the interests aroused by the Academy were very much alive.

But, for the University Art Collections, the really important student of the Foulis's era was William Hunter (1718–1783), anatomist, obstetrician, and pioneer of medical education. Something about Hunter's place in the London art scene and about his activities as an art collector appears in the section of this catalogue entitled 'Old Masters'. It is, however, relevant here to call attention to the diversity of his interests. His paintings, which, in this exhibition, include the Rembrandt and the Chardins, constituted only one part of his museum; other sections were devoted to the sciences of geology, zoology, ethnography, anatomy, and pathology; to a cabinet of coins rivalled in his time only by that of the King of France; and to a library of books and manuscripts which include the world-famous Hunterian (or, as it has not quite correctly been called, the York) Psalter. Without the start provided by Hunter there might never have been a

University museum and a University art collection—certainly nothing of a status comparable with that of the present Hunterian Museum.

The growth of the University's art collection is outlined in the notes which appear later in this catalogue as introductions to the different sections of the exhibition. It should, however, be said that, although the rooms in Colnaghi's have lent themselves excellently to a presentation which shows nearly all the principal aspects of the collection, much has had to be left out. In some cases the absences are not serious ones. The University has always been reluctant to look gift horses in the mouth and, if the resulting accumulation contains Rembrandt, and Chardin, and Whistler, and Mackintosh, and a large selection of prints from every era of print-making, there is also much of very dubious artistic value, ranging from less than skilful copies of well-known pictures to a painting of seagulls by Mrs Blackburn, the wife of a nineteenth-century Professor of Mathematics.

Andrew McLaren Young, GLASGOW UNIVERSITY'S
PICTURES

*   *   *

We are all under the law in our movement through life. Just as our actions in our spheres of interest are governed by our understanding of the rules, so a nation gathers to itself a system of law which is a mixture of inheritance and an absorption from the example of other nations, and always there is change as insights expand our understanding. It is invidious for a country to claim a superiority in the practice of law, since such a judgement could only be made by underestimating the character of a people. Comparative law is a recent academic activity, and one of the leading Scottish judges, Lord Cooper of Culross, commends a Frenchman for his understanding of Scottish law:

Macaulay, the great historian of England, who was himself of Scottish stock, and was, moreover, for a considerable number of years one of the members of Parliament for the city of Edinburgh, has somewhere written this phrase, "The Scot, wherever he finds himself, is bound to rise to the top as oil rises to the top of water."

The truth of this statement is demonstrated by numerous examples in all spheres of activity.

It will suffice that I recall, in literature, the names of Walter Scott and Thomas Carlyle; in science, those of James Watt and of Robert Fulton (an American, but the son of a Scotsman); in art, Raeburn the painter; in philosophy, John Stuart Mill; in economics, the sacrosanct name of Adam Smith, the father of political economy; and lastly, in the world of business, and more particularly in the world of banking and stockbroking, William Paterson, the founder of the Bank of England, and John Law, that famous Scotsman who made a notorious but unlucky attempt to introduce into France the system of those joint-stock companies which now abound everywhere.

All these names prove the truth of Macaulay's saying, and, moreover, it receives at this moment (February 1924) a new and striking confirmation in the fact that, by no means for the first time (Mr. Bonar Law is another recent example), it is a Scotsman, with a characteristically Scots name, Mr. Ramsay MacDonald, who as Prime Minister directs the destinies of the Government of Great Britain. This predominance of Scotsmen in British politics is no new thing.

The Union with England in 1707 did not involve a unification of the laws of the two countries. The Scots law has preserved a physiognomy of its own of marked originality. It owes this originality no doubt to the diverse traditions which have influenced its historical formation, and it is especially of these diverse traditions that I desire to speak briefly in this description.

For we can best obtain a general view of the Scots legal system, and of the predominant features of the private law of Scotland, by analysing the different elements which in combination have produced the Scots law of to-day. At the first blush, if I may speak frankly, the Scots law strikes us as being less important and less original than the English law.

As to importance, Scotland, according to the last Census of 1921, shows a population of only 4,882,288 inhabitants, whereas we have to include under the empire of the English law not only those persons subject to the jurisdiction of the Courts of England itself, but likewise all those under the rule of the English common law. This means almost all the English-speaking peoples; that is to say, besides England, the United States of America and the British possessions.

In that case we arrive at the imposing total of 152 millions, at which Mr. Bedwell, the secretary of the English Society of Comparative Law, estimated two years ago the number of persons subject to the English common law.

The comparison is obviously crushing for Scotland, unless, perchance, in the same way as there is a Nova Scotia, there may be in some of the British colonies a substratum of Scots law—a thing conceivable enough but which I can neither affirm nor deny.

As regards the second head of our comparison, namely, the respective originality of the two systems of law, it is perfectly true that upon three fundamental matters the English law has presented in the past, and still presents, features of originality which distinguish it profoundly from continental systems of law, whereas the Scots law, on the other hand, resembles our own as to these matters.

These three points are as follows:—

Firstly, there is an absolute divorce between the Roman law and the English law. The breach which began in the twelfth century seems to have been completed in the thirteenth soon after the date (*circa* 1214) when, under the Great Charter, the Court of Common Pleas sitting at Westminster was set up as a fixed institution.

After that time the Roman law, in consequence of events into which I cannot enter in detail, withdrew into itself, if I may so express it, confining itself to the universities and taking up a position in certain special jurisdictions, such as the Ecclesiastical Courts and, later, the Admiralty Court. In this way the Roman law preserved a very restricted authority, whereas the Courts of "Common Law," as it was called, gradually by their decisions built up a body of English law of a type quite original. I shall shew presently that nothing like this occurred in Scotland.

In the second place, the famous distinction between common law and equity which, in spite of the reforms of 1873 and 1875, still prevails in England has never existed in Scotland. Scotland, on the contrary, like France, has had from the beginning a unified law, the judges applying both law and equity.

Thirdly, the jury system in civil causes (a practice to which England by reason of her Saxon origins has remained steadily faithful) has made a profound mark upon the English law, and has contributed greatly throughout the centuries to give to English law a character quite peculiar to itself. A large number of its rules arose out of the necessity of distinguishing between law and fact, in order that, when this separation had been made, questions of fact might be laid before the jury which could pronounce upon them as "reasonable men," to use the phrase employed by our neighbours. Now, this practice of the civil jury did not exist in Scotland before the early part of the last century. The jury in civil matters was introduced there only in 1815, and, according to M. de Franqueville, it has never obtained a great success. Under the provisions of the law of 1850 the jury system in civil matters has been retained in Scotland only for the typical cases in which in England the parties cannot agree to dispense with a jury; that is to say, slander, libel, actions of damages, breach of promise of marriage, etc.

So that we have here three of the principal reasons why the English law compared with the laws of the Continent presents an appearance so markedly original, and these reasons are not applicable to the Scots law.

There is, however, one striking feature of the English law,

regarded from the French point of view, which the Scots law shares with the English law. That is the fusion of the commercial with the civil law. This fusion was brought about in England in a large degree by the energy of a Scotsman.

With us, as with most of the people of the continent of Europe, commerical law is kept separate from civil law. In England, from the end of the sixteenth and the beginning of the seventeenth century, under the influence of a famous judge, Sir Edward Coke, Chief Justice of the Court of King's Bench, the first step was taken to bring about a fusion between them. The Courts of Common Law were given competence in commercial matters, the *consuetudo mercatorum* to be applied by the civil jury as a special custom.

A century and a half later William Murray, Lord Mansfield, a famous English judge of Scottish origin and a man who had a really remarkable scientific equipment, brought about the second step in the fusion of the commercial with the civil law. He succeeded in getting the commercial law considered as a mere branch of the common law instead of as a special custom. The result of this change was that questions of commercial law were no longer left to the appreciation of juries but were decided by the judges. It was in 1765 that Lord Mansfield was able in this way to get the commercial law definitely included in the common law.

Does it follow from what I have said that, if the Scots law in its technique does not appear to us, when we compare it with our own, to present such original features as the English law does, that therefore the Scots law is of less interest to us? I am far from thinking so. On the contrary, it seems to me very regrettable that up to the present time of day we continental jurists have made no serious efforts, by addressing ourselves to the problems of which I am about to speak, to discover the causes which have produced a legal system in Scotland which is for us so full of interesting surprises.

If I were to try to put in a single sentence the characteristics of the Scots legal system, I should say: it is a law of Roman and

192

feudal origin which has been adapted in the course of eight centuries by legislation and by judicial decisions to the needs of the Scottish people, and during the last century has, little by little, been combining with the English law by a slow operation of fusion.

Four elements have combined to form the Scots law of to-day: the Roman law, the feudal law, the law of purely Scottish origin, and the English law.

Professor Henri Levy-Ullman, THE LAW OF
SCOTLAND

*   *   *

The topography of Scotland is particularly suited to one game—golf; the land is surrounded by an abundance of beaches and between these and the towns there are usually stretches of dunes and land called 'links'. It is on these links that all states of the nation participate in this game. It is of all games the most democratic, in that it embraces both sexes and spans all ages. The most famous links is at the graceful town, St Andrews. It has its own hero.

Old Tom Morris and his son, young Tom Morris, played a prominent part in golf in the period from 1850 to 1875. The father was born at St Andrews on June 16th, 1821. At the age of eighteen, he was apprenticed to Allan Robertson in the ball-making trade. When Morris was thirty years of age, Colonel Fairlie of Coodham took him to Prestwick, and he remained there until 1865, when he returned to St Andrews and became greenkeeper to the Royal and Ancient Golf Club, a position he held until 1904. Young Tom was born at St Andrews in 1851, and early exhibited remarkable powers as a golfer. At the age of sixteen he won the Open Professional Tournament at Montrose

IN MEMORY OF
"TOMMY"
SON OF THOMAS MORRIS
WHO DIED 25ᵀᴴ DECEMBER 1875 AGED 24 YEARS

DEEPLY REGRETTED BY NUMEROUS FRIENDS AND ALL GOLFERS
HE THRICE IN SUCCESSION WON THE CHAMPION'S BELT
AND HELD IT WITHOUT RIVALRY AND YET WITHOUT ENVY
HIS MANY AMIABLE QUALITIES
BEING NO LESS ACKNOWLEDGED THAN HIS GOLFING ACHIEVEMENTS

THIS MONUMENT HAS BEEN ERECTED
BY CONTRIBUTIONS FROM SIXTY GOLFING SOCIETIES

Tom Morris's Gravestone, St Andrews

against the best players in the country, and he won the Championship Belt outright by scoring three successive victories in 1868–9–70. The Championship lapsed for a year, but when it was resumed in 1872, young Tom scored his fourth successive victory. There is no doubt that young Tom was the finest golfer of his time, but the tragic death of his wife, while he was engaged playing with his father in a great golf match at North Berwick against the brothers Willie and Mungo Park, had a most depressing effect on him, and he only survived his wife a few months. Near the finish of this match a telegram reached North Berwick intimating that, following her confinement, young Tom's wife was dangerously ill. The telegram was held over by Provost Brodie and not handed to young Tom until the end of the match. The yacht of John Lewis, an Edinburgh golfer, was put at the service of the Morrises but before the party embarked, a second telegram brought the sad news to young Tom that his wife had died. It was a mournful party that made the voyage across the Forth to St Andrews. The brilliant young golfer never recovered from the shock, and he died on Christmas Day of the same year, 1875, at the age of twenty-four. There was a second son, J. O. F. Morris, who played in professional tournaments, but although a fine golfer, he never approached the brilliant execution of his elder brother. Old Tom competed in every Open Golf Championship up to and including 1896, which, curiously, was the year Harry Vardon scored his first victory in the Open Championship. Old Tom died at St. Andrews in 1908. He was respected throughout the golfing world for his honest, sturdy qualities. His portrait hangs in the Royal and Ancient Clubhouse, and the home green at St Andrews is named in his memory. A monument, with a sculptured figure of Young Tom, in golfing pose, was erected by public subscription in St Andrews Cathedral Churchyard and a smaller memorial stone was placed on the grave when old Tom died.

It is possible to claim ever since Zhdanov's proclamation of the doctrine of socialist realism at the First Writers' Congress in the Soviet Union in 1934 that although not a communist, the first socialist-realist poet in Scotland was William McGonagall.

An Address to the New Tay Bridge

Beautiful new railway bridge of the Silvery Tay,
With your strong brick piers and buttresses in so grand array,
And your thirteen central girders, which seem to my eye
Strong enough all windy storms to defy.
And as I gaze upon thee my heart feels gay,
Because thou are the greatest railway bridge of the present day,
And can be seen for miles away
From north, south, east, or west of the Tay
On a beautiful and clear sunshiny day,
And ought to make the hearts of the "Mars" boys feel gay,
Because thine equal nowhere can be seen,
Only near by Dundee and the bonnie Magdalen Green.

Beautiful new railway bridge of the Silvery Tay,
With thy beautiful side-screens along your railway,
Which will be a great protection on a windy day,
So as the railway carriages won't be blown away,
And ought to cheer the hearts of the passengers night and day
As they are conveyed along thy beautiful railway,
And towering above the silvery Tay,
Spanning the beautiful river shore to shore
Upwards of two miles and more,
Which is most wonderful to be seen
Near by Dundee and the bonnie Magdalen Green.

Thy structure to my eye seems strong and grand,
And the workmanship most skilfully planned;
And I hope the designers, Messrs Barlow & Arrol, will prosper for
    many a day
For erecting thee across the beautiful Tay.

And I think nobody need have the least dismay
To cross o'er thee by night or by day,
Because thy strength is visible to be seen
Near by Dundee and the bonnie Magdalen Green.

Beautiful new railway bridge of the Silvery Tay,
I wish you success for many a year and a day,
And I hope thousands of people will come from far away,
Both high and low without delay,
From the north, south, east, and the west,
Because as a railway bridge thou are the best;
Thou standest unequalled to be seen
Near by Dundee and the bonnie Magdalen Green.

And for beauty thou art most lovely to be seen
As the train crosses o'er thee with her cloud of steam;
And you look well, painted the colour of marone,
And to find thy equal there is none,
Which, without fear of contradiction, I venture to say,
Because you are the longest railway bridge of the present day
That now crosses o'er a tidal river stream,
And for beauty thou art most lovely to be seen
Near by Dundee and the bonnie Magdalen Green.

The New Yorkers boast about their Brooklyn Bridge,
But in comparison to thee it seems like a midge,
Because thou spannest the silvery Tay
A mile and more longer I venture to say;
Besides the railway carriages are pulled across by a rope,
Therefore Brooklyn Bridge cannot with thee cope;
And as you have been opened on the 20th day of June,
I hope Her Majesty Queen Victoria will visit thee very soon,
Because thou are worthy of a visit from Duke, Lord, or Queen,
And strong and securely built, which is most worthy to be seen
Near by Dundee and the bonnie Magdalen Green.

William McGonagall

Girls at Play, by John Quentin Pringle

A kind of Scottish artist:

John Quinton Pringle 1864–1925   *Girls at Play*

Pringle is the most enigmatic of the group of artists working in Glasgow in the late nineteenth and early twentieth centuries.

Although he attended classes at the Glasgow School of Art and was a Gold Medallist in the South Kensington National Competition for life drawing in 1891, he continued in his business as an optician and watch repairer and never made a profession of painting. He rarely, if ever, exhibited in public, and had little formal contact with the Glasgow School—Macgregor, Guthrie . . . , Walton . . . , Hornel . . . , Henry . . . , and their associates. He did not sell much of his work but it is interesting to note that his patrons, and in particular William Davidson, were also patrons of Mackintosh. *Girls at Play* possesses something of the Glasgow type of Art Nouveau, with suggestions of the winsome girls of Jessie King and Annie French. But Pringle's work, especially his remarkable townscapes, is very much more substantial. He is an artist whom visitors to Scotland are repetitiously 'discovering'.

A Scots heroine—Chris Guthrie

So that was Chris and her reading and schooling, two Chris's there were that fought for her heart and tormented her. You hated the land and the coarse speak of the folk and learning was brave and fine one day; and the next you'd waken with the peewits crying across the hills, deep and deep, crying in the heart of you and the smell of the earth in your face, almost you'd cry for that, the beauty of it and the sweetness of the Scottish land and skies. You saw their faces in firelight, father's and mother's and the neighbours', before the lamps lit up, tired and kind, faces dear and close to you, you wanted the words they'd known and used, forgotten in the far-off youngness of their lives, Scots words to tell to your heart how they rung it and held it, the toil of their days and unendingly their fight. And the next minute that passed from you,

199

you were English, back to the English words so sharp and clean and true—for a while, for a while, till they slid so smooth from your throat you knew they could never say anything that was worth the saying at all.

Lewis Grassic Gibbon, SUNSET SONG

*　　*　　*

It is a convention of modern science which I cannot aver, that in a microscopic world measurement can never be exact because what is to be measured has already been disturbed by the measurer. Scientific uncertainty reigns, which is different from normal uncertainty as experienced in life.

A compiler of a bedside book is in the same situation as the scientist. If he intrudes a personal preference the balance of his measure is disturbed. Readers may speculate as to whom of all these people lie closest to me. I do not know. But there is one person on the periphery who is close to me—because of his dryness. Henry Cockburn on the birth of a newspaper:

The year 1816 closed bitterly for the poor. There probably never were so many people destitute at one time in Edinburgh. The distress was less in severity than in 1797; but the population having increased, it was greater in extent. Some permanent good was obtained from the labour of the relieved. Bruntsfield Links were cleared of whins, and of old quarries; walks were made, for the first time, on the Calton Hill; and a path was cleared along the base of the perpendicular cliff of Salisbury Crags. Until then these two noble terraces were enjoyable only by the young and the active. . . .

The change which was taking place in the character of our population was now evinced by an occurrence which was

Finlay of Colonsay, from a Hill-Adamson calotype

remarkable both as an effect and as a cause. The first number of *The Scotsman* newspaper was published in January 1817. The incalculable importance of this event can only be understood by those who recollect that shortly before this the newspaper press of Edinburgh, though not as much fettered as in St Petersburg (as it has been said to have been), was at least in as fettered a condition as any press that is legally free could be. Most candid men who knew Scotland before the peace of 1814 will probably agree, that if the most respectable and unprosecuted London opposition newspaper had been published in Edinburgh, the editor would have been better acquainted with the Court of Justiciary than he would have found comfortable. The undisturbed continuance of the *Edinburgh Review* would be inconsistent with this statement, were it not that there is no analogy between a work of which the politics are dignified by general literature, and which only appears quarterly, at the price of five shillings, and the provocations of a cheap and purely political and generally accusative publication, tormenting every week or every day. When Major Cartwright, the itinerant reformer, lectured here about 1812, he was attended by considerable audiences; yet because he preached the doctrines of universal suffrage, and annual parliaments, no editor of any Edinburgh newspaper, though offered to be paid as for an advertisement, and one of them a hearer of the discourses, had courage to allow any account whatever of the lectures to appear in his paper. The editor who attended them told me that, though he differed from the lecturer, what he said was a good and perfectly lawful defence of the doctrines, and that he would have liked to have published their substance, but that he could not ruin his paper. He felt, and explained, that the bare exposition of such reforms would hurt the mere reporter.

The appearance therefore of a respectable opposition newspaper was hailed and condemned according to people's tastes: but they all saw in it a sign. Though only published once a week, and taking only literary advertisements, it soon attained a large circulation. It is now flourishing in a vigorous manhood,

202

immeasurably the best newspaper that exists, or has ever existed, in Scotland. Its only defect has been heaviness; a defect, however, inseparable from provincial locality, particularly in Scotland, where the people are grave, and too far out of the world to acquire smartness and tact. The original projectors of this the first Scotch newspaper which combined independence with intelligence, and moderation with zeal, were Charles Maclaren, who has since distinguished himself in science, William Ritchie, solicitor, and John Robertson, bookseller [musicseller]. Its earliest conductors were Ritchie and Maclaren, and John Ramsay Macculloch, now chiefly celebrated as a political economist, the principles of which science he has examined and disseminated with a talent and success that will make his career an era in its history. They were all able men, and honest in the public cause, the greatest virtue the conductors of a newspaper can possess. Ritchie was bold and zealous, and a very respectable legal practitioner, He died, after a tedious illness, a short time after the news of the first accession of the Whigs to real power in 1830 reached Edinburgh, when his last political act consisted in raising himself in bed on his elbow, and giving a feeble cheer.

Henry Cockburn on the first modern Musical Festival in Scotland:

The first modern Musical Festival was held in Scotland in 1815. It sprang more from charity than from love of harmony. But the music, as I am told—for though I heard some of it I did not comprehend it—was good; and the outer House, where it was performed, was not ill calculated to give it effect. We have become an infinitely more harmonious nation since then. Indeed none of our advances is more decided than our musical one. But this is not for one with deaf ears to speak of.

Henry Cockburn, MEMORIAL OF HIS TIME

203

Two places:

An Aberdeen Childhood

For Andrew Cruickshank

When the tide came to our feet in those days
there was no harm in it. The boats
sailed into the painted sky forever
but the long afternoon ended. Sea smells—
I carried them secretly in my pocket in the iron tram.
It said bad words when it hit the cassies in Constitution Street,
swore and screamed at the granite barracks at Castle Hill,
growled at Holburn, spat fire at Queen's Cross,
swayed and toppled, stuttered and slept at Rubislaw.
The daisies at the stop asked to be collected.

Every day it was this way, but for the Sabbath.
Up and down, up and down, big black Sabbath toe-caps,
boot polish under my nose. Hard to keep up with the father.
His breath wound about me in the pew,
drew me in through his wide nostrils,
out through the red lips.
Tight in my hand the warm pandrop stuck.
Would it last the two day, twenty day sermon?

The bright day stood outside, then home,
quiet as the photo. Grandma seated, Grandpa stood.
How many children?—one, two—buckle my shoe.
And the mahogany clock—tick, tock, tick, tock.
I remember.

George Bruce

The Scott Monument and Edinburgh Castle, from a Hill-
Adamson calotype

Old Edinburgh

Down the Canongate
down the Cowgate
go vermilion dreams
snake's tongues of bannerets
trumpets with words from their mouths
saying Praise me, praise me.

Up the Cowgate
up the Canongate
lice on the march
tar on the amputated stump
Hell speaking with the tongue of Heaven
a woman tied to the tail of a cart.

And history stands by a dark entry
with words from his mouth
that say Pity me, pity me
but never forgive.

Norman MacCaig, A MAN IN MY POSITION

*　　*　　*

For the Scotsman to hear a piper on a quiet day practising in the distance is to recognise a fundamental quality of his environment, that dimension of it which comes from the Highlands. Queen Victoria noted what Dr Norman MacLeod of the Barony had to say about this:

The music of the Highlands is the pibroch of the great war-pipe, with its fluttering pennons, fingered by a genuine Celt, in full Highland dress, as he slowly paces a baronial hall, or amidst the wild scenery of his native mountains. The bagpipe is the instrument best adapted for summoning the clans from the far-off glens to rally round the standard of their chiefs, or for leading a Highland regiment to the attack amidst the roar of battle. The pibroch is also constructed to express a welcome to the chief on his return to his clan, and to wail out a lament for him as he is borne by his people to the old burial-place in the glen or in the sainted Isle of Graves. To those who understand its carefully composed music, there is a pathos and depth of feeling suggested by it which a Highlander alone can fully sympathise with; associated by him as it always is with the most touching memories of his home and country; recalling the faces and forms of the departed; spreading forth before his inward eye panoramas of mountain, loch, and glen, and reviving impressions of his early and happiest years. And thus, if it excites the stranger to laughter, it excites the Highlander to tears, as no other music can do, in spite of the most refined culture of his after life. It is thus, too, that what appears to be only a tedious and unmeaning monotony in the music of the genuine pibroch, is not so to one under the magic influence of Highland associations. There is, indeed, in every pibroch a certain monotony of sorrow. It pervades even the "welcome," as if the young chief who arrives recalls the memory of the old chief who has departed. In the "lament" we naturally expect this sadness; but even in the "summons to battle," with all its fire and energy, it cannot conceal what it seems already to anticipate, sorrow for the slain. In the very reduplication of its hurried notes, and in the repetition of its one idea, there are expressions of vehement passion and of grief—"the joy of grief," as Ossian terms it, which loves to brood upon its own loss, and ever repeats the one desolate thought which fills the heart, and which in the end again breaks forth into the long and loud agonising cry with which it began. All this will no doubt seem both meaningless and extravagant to many, but it is nevertheless a deliberate expressed conviction.

Frank Adam, THE CLANS, SEPTS AND REGIMENTS OF
THE SCOTTISH HIGHLANDS

Two views of war:

When will the war be by?

"This year, neist year, sometime, never,"
A lonely lass, bringing hame the kye,
Pu's at a floo'er wi' a weary sigh,
An' laich, laich, she is coontin' ever
"This year, neist year, sometime, never,
When will the war be by?"

"Weel, wounded, missing', deid,"
Is there nae news o' oor lads ava?
Are they hale an' fere that are hine awa'?
A lass raxed oot for the list, to read—
"Weel, wounded, missing', *deid*";
An' the war was by for twa.

Charles Murray, HAMEWITH AND OTHER POEMS

Warriors

> "O arms that arm, for a child's wars, the child!"
> RANDALL JARRELL

Though never in the wards of the hospital for
Disabled servicemen at Erskine—First World War—
I saw an old man wheelchaired through its Park one night
By an old man who was blind. The candles were alight
On chestnut trees, a lame destroyer on the Clyde
Was being nursed by tugs against the highest tide
Of May to its dismantlement. The wheelchaired man
Was watching, too, telling his friend, that veteran
And blinded one, all that was going on. No shock
Of pride or pity moved me then. Dumbarton Rock
Rose in the dusk, my own Gibraltar. History
Was everywhere as forts and battles, conscripting me.

My mother went to Erskine once with ladies from
Inchinnan Women's Guild. In bed when she came home,
I heard her tell my father how moved she'd been by these
Blinded basketweavers and nimble amputees.
In my imagination, there is a special place
For that night, for that Park, and for the expert face
Of the man in the wheelchair, and his friend who was blind.
If that is wrong, or nearly patriotic, I don't mind.
To me it's neither. For they had suffered all that gore
We played at, and made me see that as a guilty war,
A childhood. Neither willingness or wounds would lead
Me to them from the field. In no war would I bleed.

Douglas Dunn

Ben Nevis

Ben Nevis, reaching a height of 4,400 feet above sea level, is the highest mountain in the British Isles, being rather more than 100 feet higher than Ben MacDhui, chief of the Cairngorm range. It stands at the head of Loch Linnhe, in Lochaber.

The derivation of the name Nevis is uncertain. The Gaelic name of the hill is Beinn Nimheis, and popular tradition describes it as the Hill of Heaven. The river Nevis probably named the hill, and Professor Watson is inclined to believe that the name is identical with the Old Irish "neim," and may mean the "venomous one." Glen Nevis and its river had a bad reputation in old days. A sixteenth-century bard writes of Glen Nevis:

> "Glen Nevis, a glen of stones,
>   A glen where corn ripens late,
>   A long, wild, waste glen,
>   With thievish folk of evil habit."

It has also been written of as "a glen on which God has turned His back."

The old people were awed by the darkness and gloom of Glen Nevis, from which the Ben towers mightily to the clouds. The pastime of mountaineering was then unknown, and it must have been rare indeed for any man to have climbed the hill. Then came the time when an observatory was built on the summit of Ben Nevis and for the best part of half a century hourly observations, both by day and night, were made here. The observers had thrilling experiences. The winter hurricanes, sometimes blowing at a speed of over two miles a minutes, threatened to sweep them, with the furiously driven snow, over the great precipice that dropped sheer from beside the observatory. The record of one of the observers (*Forty Years on Ben Nevis*, by W. M. Kilgour) is a book which all who love the Scottish hills should read, and it sometimes recalls the Everest expedition on a smaller scale.

Northern Lights, St. Elmo's Fire, Glories, Fire-balls, wonderful rainbows spanning the heavens, the blackness of an approaching storm, all these things were watched with appreciation by the small band who lived together in their mountain fastness on the Roof of Scotland.

The observatory, alas, has been abandoned, but it was built so firmly that it should stand for many a day. Its reports in these days of flying would be of considerable value, for it stands in the path of the storms which approach us from the Atlantic.

One summer night that I spent on the summit of Ben Nevis remains as a clear memory. When I reached the plateau the sun had already set in the glens beneath me, but the hill-top was still bathed in its last rays, and the lingering snow-fields were faintly pink in its glow. The low sun passed just above the Cuillin summits in distant Skye, so that their jagged peaks stood out in sharp relief, and finally sank below the horizon beyond the hills of Knoydart. For fully three-quarters of an hour after the sun had set its rays still shot high into the northern sky, and throughout the short night the horizon west and north held the afterglow, while in the east a waning moon struggled to pierce the mist with her silvery rays.

By dawn the face of the landscape had changed. During the brief hours of dusk a pall of white mist, creeping stealthily west from the distant North Sea, had covered all the highlands. From this vast sea of mist the tops of the highest hills rose clearly. Never, either before or since, have I seen so unusual and wonderful a sight. Before the sun rose upon it the mist was grey and cold. Very gently the sun warmed that ocean of mist, so that a rose-coloured glow suffused it. On this glowing aerial sea the shadow of the Ben was thrown for many miles towards the southwest. On the hill-top scarcely a breath of wind stirred, but several thousand feet below me the cloud moved westward, and during its slow journey towards the Atlantic assumed in places the form of gigantic billows which rose above the average level of the mist sea as they flowed over some insignificant hill that barred their way.

Even at ten o'clock the vast cloud canopy was still unbroken, and now reflected the rays of the sun with brilliance. High above the mist to the east the Cairngorm Hills were visible; Cairn Toul (4,241 feet) being especially prominent across fifty miles of the Scottish highlands. To the southward of it LochnaGar, on the King's Forest of Balmoral, climbed above the cloud. Of all the peaks rising from the misty sea, Schiehallion, "fairy Hill of the Caledonians," was the most striking, its tapering cone rising grandly to the blue of the sky. West, the two peaks of Cruachan just topped the cloud, but here the level of the mist was higher, and hid all but the summits of the highest hills. Sgùrr a' Mhaim, across Glen Nevis, raised its crater-shaped corrie to the bright sunshine, and through my glass I saw two stags reach its ridge, and look down into the white ocean of cloud beneath them.

There are few flowering plants on the plateau of Ben Nevis, for the season of growth here is a very short one, but a small colony of plants of the starry saxifrage (*saxifraga stellaris*) flower here at an elevation of 4,300 feet above the sea. This is, I believe, the highest point at which any flowering plants are found in Britain, for it is slightly higher than the summit of Ben MacDhui, where the cushion pink (*silene acaulis*) is found.

I have stood on the summit of Ben Nevis on fine clear days, yet I have still to look forward to seeing the hills of the northern coast of Ireland. The distance is so great that it is only very occasionally that these distant hills are visible. The observatory staff have placed it on record that they CAN be seen on days of extreme visibility.

The climb I have described was in the middle of July—at the height of summer. Another day on which I climbed the Ben was in May. Summer that year came early to Lochaber. The birches, swaying their young green leaves in the soft breeze, were happy in the warmth of the sun. Fields of wild hyacinths scented the air. Only on the brow of Ben Nevis did winter linger. Down in Glen Nevis the river flowed low and clear. Glen Nevis is on the eastern border of Fort William. The climber takes the road up the east side of the glen, and at a farm-house finds the beginning of the path to the hill-top. The ascent is easy and daring spirits have even driven motor-cars and motor bicycles to the summit of the Ben, but this is not to be recommended. The ordinary mortal will be thankful if he reaches by his own unaided power the highest land in the British Isles.

As I climbed, this May day, Ben Nevis seemed to tower to the blue sky, and the strong sun gleamed on its great snow-fields. The bleating of lambs was heard. Beside the springs of clear water the green leafy rosettes of the starry saxifrage took the place of the pink flowers of the lousewort which had been seen at lower levels. On the path a ptarmigan's feather lay, but no voice of bird was heard that day upon the Ben which rose, grim and mighty, from a flower-strewn base.

From the half-way hut the view was already remarkable. Delicately pencilled on the north-west horizon rose Rhum. In the middle foreground was Loch Eil, its waters pale blue and calm. A herring drifter steamed out from the Caledonian Canal, and steered away for the open sea and the summer herring fishing in the Isles. I continued to climb, and at the 3,500 feet level entered the country of the snows. At first the snow lay in small fields, but before I had arrived at a height of 4,000 feet I was walking across an unbroken expanse of glistening white. Ben Nevis, like most hills, is deceptive. The summit appears close at hand and the climber is cheered. But now, as he thinks to stand on the summit, yet another snowy slope rises ahead of him, and this too must be surmounted, painfully and slowly, if the snow be soft. Many insects rested on the snow-cap. The warm wind had carried them up from the lower slopes and they had alighted on an inhospitable waste. Across the snow they crept. After sunset they would have neither the power to rise nor the knowledge where to fly to escape the frost, and few would survive the night. Across the abyss of Glen Nevis Sgùrr a' Mhaim rose. Its eastern crater-shaped corrie where I had seen the two stags on a midsummer day years before was now filled with unbroken snow. Bidean nam Beann, highest of Argyllshire hills, rose from dark Glen Coe, and near it was Beinn Bhéir.

Great clouds, inky-black and menacing, approached the plateau of Ben Nevis. They hid the sun: they curled and eddied, with primrose edges and awe-inspiring centres. A twilight fell on the Ben. From white, the snows changed to pale grey and themselves appeared intangible and cloud-like. Across this Arctic waste rose a line of stone cairns that used to guide the observers to the summit in mist and snow, in the days when the observatory was occupied. At last I was close to the hill-top. Along the precipice a great cornice of snow extended into space. It was impossible to know whether I was standing above firm ground or was suspended by the frozen snow over an abyss of 2,000 feet. No Arctic tundra could have been more lonely. There must have been an average depth of twelve feet of snow on the hill-top. Yet in the glen beneath me the birches were in leaf, and violets and wild hyacinths were growing among the uncurling bracken fronds.

From the unbroken snowy surface the flat roof of the abandoned observatory and its chimney projected a few inches. The roof might have been a large flat rock. It was sun-warmed and pleasant to sit upon. Here I rested, looking over a wide country of hill, glen and sea, smiling and sun-lit.

West and north rose hill upon hill. Beyond Lismore, low and green, was the Isle of Mull. Its highest hill, Beinn Mhór, was the only peak, north, south, east and west, on which a cloud rested. Beyond the cliffs of Gribun in Mull I fancied I could make out Iona. Far beyond Ben Resipol of Ardnamurchan rose the isles of Coll and Tiree on the hazy Atlantic. A hundred miles distant from where I sat were the hills of South Uist in the Outer Hebrides. Hecla, Corodale, the long ridge of Beinn Mhór—all were distinct. Bearing north, the Cuillin hills formed the horizon. So clear was the air in this direction that each sharp top could be distinguished.

Upon Sgùrr nan Gillean a snow-field shone. The glass showed the Inaccessible Pinnacle of Sgùrr Dearg rising black against the sky. Even the great cairn on the summit of Beinn na Cailliche was visible. A sea of primrose mist, drifting before a northerly wind, swirled about the slopes of Glamaig. To the south the view was not so clear. Schiehallion was seen, but was less imposing than she had been on that early morning when I had watched the sun shine upon the aerial sea. To the east the Cairngorms were in strong sunshine. Cairn Toul I recognised, and Brae Riach with its snow-filled corrie, and, across the depths of Lairig Ghru, the shoulder and summit of Ben MacDhui. It is a far cry from Iona, Coll and the Outer Hebrides to Schiehallion and the Cairngorms—from Jura (seen on the horizon southward) to the Cuillin of Skye and the hills of Ross-shire.

The ascent of Ben Nevis had been arduous. The descent was swift and easy. Down 2,000 feet of the hill I was able to follow a snow-filled gulley. The gradient was so steep that it would have been scarcely possible to have descended here under ordinary conditions, and at times I seemed in danger of disappearing over a snowy precipice. The snow, however, was soft and gave excellent footing. I heard beneath my feet the rush of a hill torrent, flowing unseen through a snow tunnel. The snow was blinding in the intensity of its light. I glissaded quickly down this almost vertical snow slope, and as I moved had the curious illusion of being suspended in space. Near the half-way hut I came upon the path and here, looking back, I saw great thunder-clouds gathering above the Ben, but the lower slopes of the hill were in brilliant sunshine.

That night, from the birches of Loch Eil, I looked back on to Ben Nevis. Above the lesser hills it towered, massive and imposing. In the evening light the great cornice fringing its summit was lemon-tinted. The lower slopes, snowless and in shadow, were of a deep blue. A thunder-cloud lay beyond the summit of glowing snow. Thus Ben Nevis appeared at the coming of summer. In June the snows on its crown gradually lessen, and disappear in July, but there is one snow-field in the north-east corrie which has never been known to melt, and they say in Lochaber that if snow should disappear from the Ben, the hill would revert to the Crown.

Seton Gordon, HIGHWAYS AND BYWAYS IN
THE WEST HIGHLANDS

*   *   *

It has often been repeated that the Kirk killed the theatre in Scotland. This is not strictly true. The Establishment has always tried to censor the theatre everywhere, whether in Greece, Rome, England or France. The fact is that the theatre by its ingenuity has managed to circumvent censorship. Aristophanes, Shakespeare and Racine in their different ways are witness to that. In saying that up until now Scotland has not produced a great dramatist is to confess two things: that great drama happens very infrequently, and that when it happens it creates its own conditions to surmount the censorship. More later.

In one sphere, the Scottish theatre was superb—the Scots comic: Lauder, Fyffe, Tommy Lorne hovered on the verge of caricature and fantasy appropriate to a nation that like the Greeks had to remind themselves always when tempted to extreme expression 'nothing too much'. Even the Scots comic knew this. Will Fyffe, perhaps the middle one between Lauder the romantic and Lorne the fantastic, did this best. A Fyffe study:

The Scot's Lament

I'm Scotch and I'm married, two things I can't help,
    I'm married—but I have no wife—

For she bolted and left me—but that's nothing new,
    It happens sa often in life.
So I journeyed ta London, for that's where she'd gone
    With her lover to hide her disgrace.
And though London's a big town I swore I'd not rest
    Till I'd searched every street in the place.
And I tramped—how I tramped—weary mile upon mile
    Till exhausted and ready ta drop.
I would not give in, so I climbed on a bus,
    And took a front seat on the top.
We came to a halt in a brightly lit square
    To my joy, there ma lassie I spied,
Looking weary and worn, but thank heaven—ALONE—
    From my heart—"Maggie—Maggie" I cried.
She gasped with delight as I rose from ma seat,
    But a harrowing thought made me wince,
I couldna get off—for I'd just paid ma fare,
    AND I'VE NEVER CAUGHT SIGHT OF HER SINCE.

Kitty Kennedy Allen and Kennedy Allen, THE OLD
TIME STAR'S BOOK OF MONOLOGUES

Great theatre is very difficult to accomplish. Only Greece, England, France and Norway have provided Europe with a great innovating theatre. James Bridie was initially a doctor whose name was Osborne Mavor; one of his jokes was that Ibsen was really a Scots dramatist named Henry Gibson. Bridie stayed in Scotland, and founded the Citizen's Theatre in Glasgow. His counterpart was Barrie, who went to London and success. Bridie had the metaphysical element, the lack of which Buchan detected in Scott. It will become an essential feature of Scottish theatre. I don't think it would ever have occurred to Barrie to write the following Preface:

217

The Anatomy of Failure

This time, I am going to gossip about these plays, not explain them. I do not make this choice from idleness. It is easier to yield to temptation than to resist it.

A play is more vulnerable to misunderstanding than is any other branch of rhetoric. It is terrible to an author to be misunderstood. He is always a little *entêté* in the presence of his own works. You have heard a tipsy man in full tide. He yearns to be understood. He explains himself point by point. At all costs his thoughts must be made clear, and attention must be drawn to the beauty and subtlety with which he has expressed these inspired things.

He becomes a bore. His lyric state is not the state in which good, sharp, explanatory criticism is evolved. He is, if possible, shut up. So let it be with me, If it had been intended that I should tell what I had to tell in essays, as essays they would have appeared. As to their meaning, that will no doubt be made plain after I am dead, in University Extension Lecture Courses. If not, if their meaning is never made plain, I hope it will be nothing to me. I shall either have more important things to think about or I shall be nothing myself. So, for the moment, I shall confine myself to gossip about these plays.

I cannot, however, resist one short, parenthetic piece of explanation. The mention of tipsy men put it into my head.

An Irish Critic, who has made himself quite ill by trying to conceal (under jovial phrases) his contempt for and antipathy to most of my recent work, has taken me and good Mr. Linklater to task for glorifying the Scottish Sot.

You will find that a great deal of imitation rum, gin, beer, orange curacoa and sherry is drunk in these plays, and that the hero of each of them gets blotto at least once during the action. This might be taken to indicate that I like my heroes to be drunk and think them attractive in this condition. Indeed, this is not so. It is a trick. It is a legitimate trick if it is cleverly introduced—that is to say, if it is natural to the action that the player should pretend to

218

be drunk; and if he is not compelled to commit any offensive act or say any offensive thing. Getting drunk is not in itself necessarily an offensive act.

The point of the trick is that in my part of the country a man is slow in revealing the picturesque or emotional side of his nature unless he has blunted his inhibitions by some artificial means. Now, in a stage play an audience must be enabled to size up a character as quickly as a boxer sizes up his enemy in the ring. The actor must unbosom himself rapidly and all of a heap if he is to establish the philosophy underlying the motives of his two hours' traffic. In the old plays a confidant was used. To a drunken man, all the world is his confidant. It is a good little trick, but I shall be careful, in future, not to overwork it. Nevertheless, I have been less bethumped by the experts for it than for reviving the soliloquy (in *The Black Eye*); and I take it that they have left me alone because the trick succeeded. In others words, it escaped attention.

Now that I have disclaimed any attempt to evangelise the Bottle, I may be permitted to do what I set out to do—to fill my Preface with innocuous gossip about the plays contained in this book.

It would be idle to pretend to you that these plays were ever what is called a "success.' *Mary Read*, it is true, scored her hundred performances; but in doing so she lost a sum of five figures to her promoters. *The Black Eye* began vigorously but died in the sixties. *Marriage is no Joke* ran for five nights.

It is interesting to speculate why they failed. Each of them started with initial advantages. To begin with, they are not bad plays. Many worse have won fame and fortune for everybody concerned in their production. Then, they were presented under the several auspices of Sir Barry Jackson, Mr. C. B. Cochran and Mr. Alexander Korda, three very intelligent and expert persons. Two plays were directed by Mr. H. K. Ayliff, one by Mr. Tyrone Guthrie. They were brilliantly performed by artists who had already reached the front rank of their profession. In short, and in the words of the contract, they were "performed in a first-rate

219

manner in West End Theatres." *Mary Read* was received with enthusiasm by the Press; *The Black Eye*, certain Critics dissenting, also with enthusiasm; *Marriage is no Joke* with generosity. Only one Critic—a lady who detested *The Black Eye*—used the only word that can damn a play. She found it dull.

The only nigger boys left in the wood pile are the Author and his Audience—or rather The Public, who stayed away or failed to incite their friends to attend. As the customer is always right, the Author is left alone.

Had he made his plays too recondite for the Public? No. For much more complicated plays had pleased them enormously. Was their workmanship gimcrack? No. For if it had been, the three impresarios would not have bought them, any more than they would have bought bad furniture or bad pictures. Were they indecent, blasphemous or affronting to the Monarch and his Lieges? No. For if they had been, Lord Cromer would not have allowed them. Were they inconsonant with the fashion? No. For the fashion is always ready to admit fairy tales and adventure stories. *Mary Read* was Diana, Hippolyta, Imogen, Rosalind and Peter Pan rolled into one with a dash of Joan of Arc. *Marriage is no Joke* had the essence of all the stories of bull-headed fighting men from Hercules to John L. Sullivan. "George" in *The Black Eye* was all the younger sons and Idle Jacks out of Grimm, and his story was their story. Short of making a play about Cinderella, I could not have been more in the fashion.

What, then, was the matter with the plays? In what manner had I made their attractive themes and attractive presentations unattractive to the Public? I will tell you. In each case I only discovered the essential fault after it was too late; but it will be a happiness to know that the bitterness of these defeats may be a warning to others.

A. *Marriage is no Joke*. This most complete of all my failures I have analysed in a book of essays—itself a failure, so I can quite decently quote from it.

Our people (I suggested) *have a habit of looking at both sides of*

220

a halfpenny. In a recent play (I went on) *this trait was fully tested. The play divided itself into two parts. In one, a Highland divinity student was represented as making a beast of himself with rum; entering, under a cloud of alcoholic verbiage, into a frivolously undertaken marriage contract; stupefying himself with drink on his wedding night; committing a dangerous and brutal assault upon a servant; and, later, handing over the entire control of his destiny to a half-educated, underbred, little hussy of a wife.*

The audience (I continued) *took the squalid scene in the public-house and the debasing and sordid scene in the bridal chamber as pieces of entertaining, naturalistic, sentimental comedy, and greeted them with a ripple of happy laughter that was music to their thaumaturgist's ears. They took the bombastic brute of a hero and his ill-tempered vixen to their hearts. If the play had all been in this vein of pleasantry it might have succeeded. . . .*

The first part (I said) *was written in a fantastic, deliberately unreal manner, otherwise it would have been quite unbearable. In Part Two it was necessary to precipitate the "hero" into a wilder form of life in which his savage instincts could follow their bent in a grotesque sort of world. I chose an unfamiliar field of the War and, to avoid tumbling into absurdity, based every single incident, every word spoken, almost, on something that had really happened. I presented these incidents with the utmost restraint. Lest the chief protagonist, a woman, should appear incredible, I drew her straight from life. I was accused of stealing her from a melodrama. Part Two was regarded as a wild, unbridled dash into impossible theatricality. And down came the play like a sack of coals, never to rise again. The Public had turned round the halfpenny.*

That is what I said. Allowing for the affectation that comes out all over me in spots when I try to write prose, that is still my opinion. I told the audience lies and they believed me. There was nothing in the world to prevent their believing me when I told the truth. But they were English, and they wouldn't.

B. *Mary Read.* Miss Flora Robson was one day taking tea with my wife and me. She was mourning over a procession of tortured spinsters leading to the crack of Doom. She foresaw that she would be expected by London managements to play them all. I remembered that she had played a little short part in a play of mine, once, and had given a performance of such appalling beauty that she burst the play in two. I said, "Would you like to play Mary Read?" And she said, "Who is Mary Read?" And I said, "She was a Pirate." And Miss Robson said, "Yes. I should like to play a pirate." So I set to and wrote the play.

I made a picaresque thing with thirty or forty Smolletish characters casting their many-coloured beams on a statuesque Mary. Then I found out that it wasn't, and my friends and advisers thought it wasn't, a PLAY. Mary didn't move. She didn't develop—though why characters should be expected to develop in a play when they don't in real life, I cannot tell you. The play's back broke in the middle. Her soldier lover—a hobbledehoy recruit in the old version—was shot dead in the barn; and her sailor lover was a cynical brute. She had great games with Spanner, the One-Legged Sailor, Captain Tappit, Rackham, Ann Bonney, Corner and the rest; but there was no Plot. It obviously wouldn't hold an audience through an evening. So I asked Mr. Claud Gurney to help me. He did, and we made a play of it. Action, motive, development all began to appear. My beloved Tappits, Caseys and Ambers all fell back grumbling into their places in the scheme. The whole story was as neat as ninepence and as intelligible as the Ten Commandments. Miss Robson gave a gloriously heartening performance; Mr. Donat was excellent in the most thankless part a young star ever undertook. For we had to invent a new character to tie the broken play together. Miss Molly Macarthur achieved the feat of making the characters look as if they were wearing clothes, and not period fancy dress. There were twenty fine performances in what were left of the minor parts. The production was by the most imaginative producer of our time. But it was nobody's play. Mr. Gurney and I had done a good job, but we had cancelled out. My limp, his lisp; my way of chewing cigars, his way of pulling his moustache; my taste for pork, his for curried prawns; all had disappeared. The English will bear with a fool if he is sufficiently characteristic; but they will pass by the wisdom of the wise if the Sage is an ordinary sort of chump with no kind of headmark. They insist on seeing the label, and the dog had licked off the direction. If he had been my dog, he wouldn't have been so good. If he had been Gurney's dog, he wouldn't have been so good. But they would have known whose dog he was and might well have loved him.

You must not think that I believe any important section of the London Public to be able to recognise the work of any author as being characteristic of that author; or that every schoolboy could catalogue the idiosyncrasies of Mr. Gurney or of Mr. Bridie. Far from it. But the Public likes work to be idiosyncratic and *Mary Read* is not that.

There is one further point. Some readers of this play may be puzzled by a WORD pronounced, ostensibly by Mr. Earle towards the end of Act I, Scene 3. Mr. Earle says. "Yes. . . . WARNPANOTROPE!" The effect of this WORD on the Barmaid is to make her scream, "Oh, mercy me. There will be bloodshed."

I need not inform readers of *The Golden Bough* that a sect of devotees in Asia Minor advance, carrying sacrificial instruments and shouting "*Varunpanotrope*" to the ruined shrine of Dionysos in the. . . . But why should I lie to you?

It is a stage direction which has escaped the proof-reader—so boldly was it written in blue pencil by the Stage Manager—and it is such a beautiful word that the Publishers and I have let it be. And what fun for the commentators.

C. *The Black Eye*. I have left my post mortem on *The Black Eye* to the end, because here I am absolutely sure about the diagnosis and this certainty may cover some weaknesses not invisible in my earlier arguments.

The Black Eye is the best of the bunch. It failed for a reason we should all have foreseen.

The Patrons and Dictators of the Theatre are not Tired

Business Men, but their wives, daughters and lady friends. This is an axiom, and it must never be forgotten by anyone aspiring to make his mark on contemporary drama.

The Patronesses are, on the whole, fair-minded and intelligent. It is true that they are susceptible to plays that flatter their daydreams. But so are we all. If it is not invidious to take an instance, at least one very successful play owed a large proportion of its success to the persuasive statement of the untruth that the love of a good woman dispensed in suitable dosage is a great help to a medical student in getting him through his examinations. The merits of the play are not in question but there is no doubt that they were reinforced enormously by this blatant and unscrupulous piece of flattery.

On the other hand, most other kinds of humbug are rapidly detected by the woman playgoer and treated as they deserve to be treated. She can give a judgment without perpetually turning up the Book of Rules; and she troubles very little about the dramatist's opinions so long as he presents them clearly and entertainingly. If, other things being equal, she prefers to see a lovable actor in a bad play to a repellent actor in a moderately good one, why, she is quite right. She would rather have her lovable actor in a good play, and the wise impresario will see that she gets that.

One thing she can not abide; that is, to have the best side of her nature held up to ridicule. She does not go to the theatre to be insulted. *The Black Eye* was, unfortunately and quite unintentionally, a living insult to the woman playgoer.

To begin with, the play's charm is due to a pleasant male freemasonry still found uninvaded and unpurified in some clubs, pubs and dosshouses, even in 1936. Against it all decent women have waged implacable war since women began to be decent. They have won the war, but the whispers of the guerilla bands can still be heard, now and again, in waste places. That battered veteran on the run, the Serious Person, gives the password to George at the beginning of the play. His own father re-echoes it.

Sammy Samuels takes him galloping through the greenwood. Johnnie and he hoist their ridiculous flag at the final curtain.

This would be bearable if I hadn't made the women in my play advance into battle with God, commonsense and the ardour of pure affection on their side, only to retire from the field with fleas in their ears, all except the treacherous Mrs. Windlestraw, who sold the pass at the first shot. If Mrs. Windlestraw had not been impersonated by the adorable Miss Jean Cadell, I tremble to think what might have happened.

The women in *The Black Eye* are all nice women—except Mrs. Scoullar. Even Mrs. McGillivray and the Serious Person's Auntie, who do not appear, have their points. The ladies from the suburbs could have had no difficulty in identifying themselves with any one of them. They were in the right, too. Connie was right, Elspeth was right, Louie was right, Mrs. Windlestraw knew what was right, though she was too lamentably easy-going to stick up for her faith. And they were all shamefully, abominably, brutally entreated. Their sage advices were scorned, their kindly efforts set at naught. Love itself did not prevent George from following his ruinous career of folly, gambling, philosophising and alcoholism. What *right* had he to live happy ever after?

The soft answer that he had no *right* cannot turn away wrath of this calibre. Good acting, good production and, take it or leave it, good writing carried *The Black Eye* up to the General Election. Men then forgot it and Women didn't remind them of it. Quietly, firmly, without rancour or reproach, they let my play drop dead. Its ghost lingers in these pages sorry if it caused pain during its life, but still a little rebellious.

JAMES BRIDIE.

Glasgow,
    February, 1936.

*   *   *

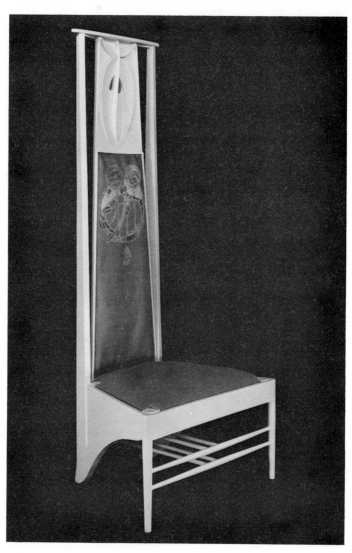

Chair, by Charles Rennie Mackintosh

226

It was in the Aberdeen Public Library that at the age of sixteen I read Thomas Hardy's Two on a Tower, *and within the year I had read all Hardy's novels borrowed from the public library. Later, I could sympathise with classical scholars at the burning of Ptolemy's library in Alexandria, and rejoice when a fragment of Aeschylus turned up in a continental library. My discovery of Hardy and the public library was, I think, due to the practical views of Andrew Carnegie:*

John Phipps, James R. Wilson, Thomas N. Miller, William Cowley—members of our circle—shared with me the invaluable privilege of the use of Colonel Anderson's library. Books which it would have been impossible for me to obtain elsewhere were, by his wise generosity, placed within my reach; and to him I owe a taste for literature which I would not exchange for all the millions that were ever amassed by man. Life would be quite intolerable without it. Nothing contributed so much to keep my companions and myself clear of low fellowship and bad habits as the beneficence of the good Colonel. Later, when fortune smiled upon me, one of my first duties was the erection of a monument to my benefactor. It stands in front of the Hall and Library in Diamond Square, which I presented to Allegheny and bears this inscription:

To Colonel James Anderson, Founder of Free Libraries in Western Pennsylvania. He opened his Library to working boys and upon Saturday afternoons acted as librarian, thus dedicating not only his books but himself to the noble work. This monument is erected in grateful remembrance by Andrew Carnegie, one of the "working boys" to whom were thus opened the precious treasures of knowledge and imagination through which youth may ascend.

This is but a slight tribute and gives only a faint idea of the depth of gratitude which I feel for what he did for me and my companions. It was from my own early experience that I decided there was no use to which money could be applied so productive of good to boys and girls who have good within them and ability and ambition to develop it, as the founding of a public library in a community which is willing to support it as a municipal institution. I am sure that the future of those libraries I have been privileged to found will prove the correctness of this opinion. For if one boy in each library district, by having access to one of these libraries, is half as much benefited as I was by having access to Colonel Anderson's four hundred well-worn volumes, I shall consider they have not been established in vain.

Andrew Carnegie, from his autobiography

*   *   *

The sun sinks in the east. The brightest sun in the galaxy that was the British Empire faded in 1947 after the Second World War. The Indian sub-continent of India and Pakistan became independent of Britain and after some argument of each other.

A great journalist visits India after 1947:

It was one of the endless discussions in the Club; so quickly they turn into lectures.

'We can't just wish away the British occupation, however much we'd like to; everywhere you look it's still there. What we can do—and we do it all the time—is offload all our shortcomings and inadequacies on British history. This is indispensable to the Indian Character. We don't do it with the same conviction as we used to, because it's beginning to look a bit silly after twenty-five years; still it's instinctive to pass the buck.

'All the same we're wholly ambivalent about the Raj. We're supposed to thank the British for giving us a public service and a system of law and at least a kind of unity. What we should be thanking them for is giving us their language, simply because it gave us access to the literature of dissatisfaction and revolt, which we simply never thought of producing for ourselves. Almost all literate Indians were exposed at some time or other to J. S. Mill and the rest of them. Obviously the only object the British had in educating us was to make us more useful clerks and babus, but as it turned out they couldn't do that without handing over the instruments of their own ultimate abolition. Frankly I don't see how they could have avoided it.

'We used our own methodology, to be sure, but the libertarian ideas were theirs, after all, and because the British ruling class is so bloody dumb they drummed this stuff into us with their exams and so on without knowing what the hell they were doing. It always seemed odd to me that your Churchill, for example, who lived on the same sort of pretentious hollow rhetoric as we do, was so taken aback and outraged by the Indian intellectual rebellion. Come to think of it, maybe he wasn't very clever at all, just brilliant.

'No, what we have against the British is that they undermined our sense of personal history—probably by accident, the way they do everything. Extraordinary how a few thousand Anglo-Saxon expatriates could brainwash millions of Indians. They encouraged us to live in the past romantically and the future competitively, so we became indifferent to our present. That wasn't difficult, of course, with the Hindu character. Our history is just a sort of myth-worship, anyhow.

'The real cruelty was that Britain robbed us of our revolution. They conned us out of our national revolution of violence, so we lost the utopian momentum of real rebellion. Since we never had that, we coasted along, we compromised. All of a sudden in 1947 we found we actually owned our own present, and we were so uneasy about it we propped up a wonderful new idea on old institutions. We inherited a bureaucracy far more English than Indian—worse, we embraced it, we cherished it, we multiplied and embellished it; to every one of its pompous bumbling ineptitudes we added more, for every opportunity for graft and nepotism we provided yet better and more crafty ones. The system was paralysed with precedents, so every year we accreted new ones. The British bequeathed us a hierarchical machinery—but, boy, when it comes to hierarchical institutions nobody can teach India anything. Today our bureaucracy is twenty times more bureaucratic, our snobberies more snobbish, our deference to the chain of command more cringing and decorous, our worship of paper more entrenched. The British created our regiments of minor ill-paid babus in the image of the Dickensian clerk and there he remains, enshrining the second-rate, terrified of decisions, passing responsibility upwards from hand to hand until it gets lost in the clouds of unseen authority.

'We have no real industralists, only speculators. We invent nothing, since it is easier to copy, and what we copy we usually demean or falsify. . . .'

Then the passion fades suddenly away, the phrases stop, the eyes cloud over, 'Bearer, tea.'

James Cameron, AN INDIAN SUMMER

Munro and Elphistone had been vindicated. It is one of the illusions of the contemporary world that liberation can only be achieved by revolution. And so the mark of revolution, the last supper of the secular state, becomes a measure of authenticity, of loyalty.

Cameron's colleague realised that he could find no refuge in reference to the revolution. To be a democrat, a person of the people and the city, is very difficult, in the diversity of the modern world.

A visitor to Edinburgh towards the end of May each year is likely to enjoy the pageantry associated with the General Assembly of the Church of Scotland. The annual assembly of the kirk, and the attendance at it of the Queen's Commissioner, are a living testimony to the historical origins of the reformed religion, to the relationship in Scotland between church and state and to the strength of the church in the country.

In Scotland the Reformation was the work not of the government of the day but of a popular movement clinched by Acts of the Scots Parliament passed during the interregnum between the death of the Queen Regent, Mary of Guise, and the return of her daughter, Mary Queen of Scots, from France in 1561. To this day, the church's assembly bears some of the marks of the sixteenth century "estates" or Parliament. The link between the assembly and the sovereign took the recognisable form of the appointment of a Commissioner by about 1580 and the series of Lord High Commissioners has continued through the centuries. In modern times the Lord High Commissioner has taken up residence in the Palace of Holyroodhouse, where he entertains church representatives and others and from where he and his lady (referred to as "Their Graces") not only attend the assembly but, with due ceremony, pay visits to good causes and deserving institutions. What was originally an act of Royal vigilance over potentially contumacious churchmen has become an occasion for mutual courtesy and the renewal of loyalty. James VI's practice of occasionally attending the assembly himself has been most happily revived by the Queen, who was present at a special assembly in 1960 to mark the 400th anniversary of the Reformation and at the regular assembly of 1970.

The members of the General Assembly are ministers and elders from parishes all over Scotland, ministers who have been "called" by their congregations and elders, men and women who have been chosen from among the congregation to assist the minister in his pastoral duties. Although the educational aims of the reformers were partly frustrated, the church has always had an educated ministry of men of independent mind drawn from all classes of society.

The church was reformed in 1560, but it was not until 1690, after long years of turmoil and bloodshed, that its method of government was finally established as presbyterian. In presbyterianism there is no hierarchy of clergy, but all ministers are equal. There is, however, a hierarchy of "courts", viz. kirk session (a meeting of the minister and elders of the individual congregation), presbytery, synod and general assembly (i.e. assembly of the whole church). A presbytery is a meeting of ministers and elders in a geographical group of parishes which superintends the parishes. For instance, a congregation's "call" to a minister must be "sustained" by the presbytery. Questions which the presbytery cannot settle are remitted to the wider grouping known as the synod and thence to the general assembly. Conversely, policy issues initiated in assembly may be "sent down" to presbyteries for consideration and report back the following year. Although autonomous and completely rooted in Scotland, the kirk is of the same family as other Reformed churches of the Continent, as distinct from the Lutheran or Anglican brands of protestantism. In both its deliberations in assembly and its parish work the Church of Scotland is deeply concerned with public issues. The language and imagery of its devotions are more evangelical than an outsider might expect of an established church. This may be traced to the influence of the dissenting presbyterians of the nineteenth century, whose evangelical fervour was in turn a reaction against the "high and dry" theology of many eighteenth-century ministers.

By organisation and by numbers—1,900 ministers and 1,100,000 communicant members—the kirk exercises a powerful influence in every part of Scotland. The Roman Catholic church also has a large membership—of about 800,000—but is less evenly distributed. Catholicism is strong in the west of Scotland and there are parts of the Highlands and Islands which were recovered for the old faith very soon after the Reformation and have held to it ever since. Individual Catholics have long played a leading part in the national life, and the Catholic community as a whole now plays a bigger part than in the past in public debate and action, often in alliance with Protestants.

The Episcopal Church in Scotland is part of the Anglican communion, but as a church it exists in its own right and has its own claim to be an inheritor of the Scottish Reformation. During the eighteenth century it was heavily penalised for its adherence to the Jacobite cause. Since its emancipation it has devoted special attention to the beauty of church buildings and of the worship offered in them.

The successors of the dissenting presbyterians who set the tone of Scottish religion in the nineteenth century were re-united (for the most part) to the established church in 1929. But unestablished, independent presbyterian churches still continue, in particular the Free Church of Scotland, which was founded by those who came out of the established church in 1843 in protest against the failure of the government to abolish the appointment of ministers by patrons. The "Wee Frees", as they are popularly called, are strong in the Highlands, and there they preserve a unique tradition of singing: metrical psalms in which the usual plain tunes are ornamented with florid arabesques. The Free Church has its own General Assembly (meeting at the same time as the Church of Scotland assembly and on the opposite side of the street) and in its public pronouncements it stands for Reformation principles against the modernising tendencies which it often sees in other churches as well as in the secular world. The other Protestant churches, such as Congregationalists (still a separate denomination in Scotland), Baptists, Methodists and the Salvation Army, also have congregations in Scotland, and from time to time have made notable contributions to the religious scene. There is a small but influential Jewish community, chiefly in Glasgow.

SCOTLAND TODAY

*   *   *

Two Scots on love:

Wedding

With a great working of elbows
The fiddlers ranted
       —Joy to Ingrid and Magnus!

With much boasting and burning
The whisky circled
       —Wealth to Ingrid and Magnus....

With deep clearings of the throat
The minister intoned
       —Thirdly, Ingrid and Magnus....

Ingrid and Magnus stared together
When midnight struck
At a white unbroken bed.

George Mackay Brown, from CONTEMPORARY
SCOTTISH VERSE

Bedtime

So put your nightdress on
It is so white and long
And your sweet night-face
Put it on also please
It is the candle-flame
It is the flame above
Whose sweet shy shame
My love, I love, I love.

Ian Hamilton Finlay, from MODERN
SCOTTISH POETRY

*   *   *

Two Great Wars in Europe and the Russian Revolution have destroyed the conventional values and structures of centuries. Mackintosh could not have foreseen in his Croall lecture that Kierkegaard would become with Marx one of the dominating thinkers of the twentieth century. Nor that Kierkegaard was a reflection in our time of Duns Scotus. In all the divinity schools of the Scottish universities there have been an existential element. John Macquarrie was at one time in Glasgow, then in the United States, and now, in Oxford.

What is Existentialism?

When we try to say what existentialism is, we are confronted with a certain elusiveness. Partly, the difficulty arises from the fact that what was intended as a serious type of philosophy has frequently been vulgarized to the level of a fad, so that the existentialist label gets applied to all sorts of people and activities that are only remotely, if at all, connected with existentialist philosophy. As Jean-Paul Sartre has written, 'the word is now so loosely applied to so many things that it no longer means anything at all.' Partly, however, the difficulty is that a kind of elusiveness is built into existentialism itself. The advocates of this philosophy deny that reality can be neatly packaged in concepts or presented as an interlocking System. The father of modern existentialism, Søren Kierkegaard, significantly named two of his most important books *Philosophical Fragments* and *Concluding Unscientific Postscript* and engaged in polemic against the all-inclusive system of Hegelian philosophy. In the existentialist view there are always loose ends. Our experience and our knowledge are always incomplete and fragmentary; only a divine Mind, if there is one, could know the world as a whole—and perhaps even for such a Mind there would be gaps and discontinuities.

But the point that existentialists have generally been critical of metaphysical systems should not be exaggerated. It does not mean that they themselves are totally unsystematic or even that some of them do not produce some kind of metaphysic of their own.

Our everyday existing is often designated by such words as *living* or *dwelling*. What does it mean to live or dwell in the world? Obviously such expressions mean much more than just being physically located in the world. Such 'location in' is certainly a part of the meaning, and later we shall give consideration to the spatiality of existence in the word. However, to live in the world is to be related to it in innumerable ways besides the spatial relation. This holds even for the way an animal lives in its world (if the expression *world* is permissible here). A whole complex branch of biology, namely, ecology, studies the nature of dwelling, the relation of the organism to that environment which forms its οἶκος or home.

The term *concern* has been used by existentialists to refer to the complex relation designated by the 'in' of being-*in*-the-world. 'Concern' is understood in a very general sense as covering the almost endless ways in which man's interests impinge on the beings around him. Handling and using, eating and drinking, building and manufacturing, finding the way, telling the time, transporting himself, sowing and reaping—these are a mere fraction of the modes of concern whereby man relates himself to his environment and harnesses it to his needs. Other activities like destroying, pushing aside, removing obstructions are also instances of concern, though these constitute its negative modes. To be in the world is to be concerned with the world, to be engaged in ceaseless interaction with the things we find within the world.

From the point of view of practical concern, therefore, a 'thing' is viewed primarily in a pragmatic way. This means in turn that the world of everyday existing is an instrumental world. A child's first question about anything is very often: 'What is it for?' The notion of a bare thing-in-itself, inert, indifferent, would seem to be a very sophisticated idea and certainly one that is remote from everyday existing. In concern, we are constantly looking around, and whatever presents itself is viewed from the perspective of practical concern and will almost certainly be pressed into service in one way or another. . . .

There is a sense in which one might say that the progress of man has consisted in the bringing of more and more items into his instrumental world. I do not mean, however, that man is at first confronted with inert, independent things to which he subsequently assigns (or in which he subsequently discovers) an instrumentality. Concern is there from the beginning. Sartre remarks: 'The thing is not first a thing in order to be subsequently an instrument; neither is it first an instrument in order to be revealed subsequently as a thing. It is an instrumental thing.'

Instruments are interlocking. They imply one another, in systems and subsystems. A pen implies paper; the paper implies a postal system; the postal system implies methods of transportation; and so on. Today, as we often hear, we live in the context of a world of immense complexity where everything seems to affect everything else. What articulates this world and gives significance to each single item within it is human concern. The everyday world is correlated with the range of human concern. This is what gives unity and system to the multifarious items embraced within the world. We see how large a part the human factor plays in constituting the everyday world, and we see also how the notion of worldhood is in a sense *a priori*, for the concept of world is already presupposed in every single instrument.

John Macquarrie, EXISTENTIALISM

*   *   *

BP's rig *Sea Quest* which discovered the Forties Field

A visitor to Scotland will be aware of the concern in this country about its destiny, and in this matter might well turn to what a poet would have in mind:

To have found one's country

To have found one's country
after a long journey
and it to be here
around one all the time.
It is like taking a girl
from the house next door,
after all that travel
that black dense wall.

To have fallen in love with
stone, thistle and strath,
to see the blood flow
in wandering old rivers,
this wound is not stanched
by handkerchiefs or verse.
This wound was after all
love and a deep curse.

Now I'm frightened to name it
lest some witch should spring
screaming out of the tombs
with a perverted broom.
I'm almost frightened to
name all the waters,
these seas, tall hills,
these misty bordered bibles.

Love's such a transient thing
except for that hard slogging
which, though it's love, we don't
name it by that ring
in which, tortured, we fight
with all the bones about us
in these cemeteries that hold
the feet in living grass.

Iain Crichton Smith, from CONTEMPORARY
SCOTTISH VERSE

Speaking of Scotland

What do you mean when you speak of Scotland?
The grey defeats that are dead and gone
behind the legend each generation
savours afresh, yet can't live on?

Lowland farms with their broad acres
peopling crops? The colder earth
of the North East? Or Highland mountains
shouldering up their rocky dearth?

Inheritance of guilt that our country
has never stood where we feel she should?
A nagging threat of unfinished struggle
somehow forever lost in the blood?

Scotland's a sense of change, an endless
becoming for which there was never a kind
of wholeness or ultimate category.
Scotland's an attitude of mind.

Maurice Lindsay, THE RUN FROM LIFE

An invocation, a hope, a blessing for this people and their land, as the northern lights come up at the end of the day:

The Heart Could Never Speak

The heart could never speak
But that the Word was spoken.
We hear the heart break
Here with hearts unbroken.
Time, teach us the art
That breaks and heals the heart.

Heart, you would be dumb
But that your word was said
In time, and the echoes come
Thronging from the dead.
Time, teach us the art
That resurrects the heart.

Tongue, you can only say
Syllables, joy and pain,
Till time, having its way,
Makes the word live again.
Time, merciful lord,
Grant us to learn your word.

Edwin Muir, COLLECTED POEMS

Bibliography

Adam, Frank, *The Clans, Septs and Regiments of the Scottish Highlands* (Johnston & Bacon, 1970)

Bliss, Trudy (ed), *Thomas Carlyle: Letters to His Wife* (Victor Gollancz, 1953)

Bridie, James, *Moral Plays, and a preface, 'The Anatomy of Failure'* (Constable, 1936)

Brower, R. A. (ed), *On Translation* (Harvard University Press, 1959)

Buchan, John, *Montrose* (Hodder & Stoughton, 1928)

Buchan, John, *Sir Walter Scott* (Cassell, 1932)

Cameron, James, *An Indian Summer* (Macmillan, 1974)

Carlyle, Alexander (ed), *New Letters and Memorials of Jane Welsh Carlyle* (Bodley Head, 1903)

Carnegie, A., *Autobiography of Andrew Carnegie* (Constable, 1920)

Carswell, Catherine, *The Life of Robert Burns* (Chatto & Windus, 1930)

Cockburn, Henry, *Memorials of His Time* (T. N. Foulis, 1910)

Corss, James, *Uranoscopia: the Contemplation of the Heavens in a Perpetual Speculum, or General Prognostication for Ever* (A Society of Booksellers, Edinburgh, 1662)

Declaration of Arbroath, 1320, The (HMSO, 1970)

Dunn, Douglas, 'Warriors', *Encounter* (March, 1976)

Duns, John, *Memoir of Sir J. Y. Simpson, Bart* (Edmenston & Douglas, 1873)

Fisher, H. A. L., *Biography of Viscount Bryce* (Macmillan, 1927)

Galt, John, *The Member*, ed Ian A. Gordon (Scottish Academic Press, 1975)

Gibbon, Edward, *Autobiography of Edward Gibbon* (Oxford University Press, 1907)

Gibbon, Lewis Grassic, *Sunset Song* (Hutchinson, 1946)

Glazebrook, Sir Richard Tetley, *James Clerk Maxwell and Modern Physics* (Cassell, 1896)

Golfer's Handbook (Munro-Barr Publications, 1977)

Gordon, Seton, *Highways and Byways in the West Highlands* (Macmillan, 1935)

Hogg, James, *The Three Perils of Man: War, Women and Witchcraft*, ed Douglas Gifford (Scottish Academic Press, 1972)

Hume, David, *Enquiries concerning the Human Understanding and concerning the Principles of Morals*, ed L. A. Selby-Bigge (Oxford, Clarendon Press, 1902)

242

Innes of Learney, Sir Thomas, *The Tartans of the Clans and Families of Scotland* (Johnston & Bacon, 1971)

James Clerk Maxwell: a commemoration volume, 1831–1931 (Cambridge University Press, 1931)

King, Agnes Gardner, *Kelvin the Man* (Hodder & Stoughton, 1925)

Kinghorn, A. M., and Law, A. (eds), *The Poems of Allan Ramsay and Robert Ferguson* (Scottish Academic Press, 1974)

Lauder, Sir Thomas Dick, *An Account of the great Floods of August 1829, in the Province of Moray, and adjoining districts* (Adam Black, 1830)

Levy-Ullmann, Henri, 'The Law of Scotland', *Juridical Review*, 370 (1925)

Lindsay, Maurice (ed), *Modern Scottish Poetry: An Anthology of the Scottish Renaissance* (Faber, 1966)

Lindsay, Maurice, *The Run from Life* (Cygnet Press, 1975)

Livingstone, David, *Missionary Travels and Researches in South Africa* (John Murray, 1857)

Ludovici, L. J., *Fleming: Discoverer of Penicillin* (Andrew Dakers, 1952)

McAlister, Gilbert, *James Maxton: The Portrait of a Rebel* (John Murray, 1935)

MacCaig, Norman, and Scott, Alexander (eds), *Contemporary Scottish Verse, 1959–1969* (Calder & Boyars, 1970)

MacCaig, Norman, *A Man in My Position* (Hogarth, 1969)

McGonagall, William, *Poetic Gems* (Duckworth, 1955)

Mackie, J. D., *History of Scotland* (Penguin, 1964)

Mackintosh, H. R., *Types of Modern Theology* (Fontana, 1964)

Macquarrie, John, *Existentialism* (Penguin, 1973)

Marchand, Leslie A. (ed), *In My Hot Youth*, Byron's Letters and Journals, vol 1 (John Murray, 1973)

Mary Queen of Scots, *The Last Letter of Mary Queen of Scots* (HMSO, 1975)

Morgan, Edwin, *Wi the Haill Voice* (Carcanet Press, 1972)

Muir, Edwin, *Collected Poems* (Faber, 1960)

Murray, Charles, *Hamewith and Other Poems* (Constable, 1929)

O'Brien, Brian, *She Had a Magic* (Jonathan Cape, 1958)

Old Time Stars' Book of Monologues, The (Reynolds Music, 1929)

Oxford Book of Scottish Verse, The, chosen by J. MacQueen and Tom Scott (Oxford, Clarendon Press, 1966)

Proust, Marcel, *Cities of the Plain*, pt 1, Remembrance of Things Past, vol 7, trans. C. K. Scott-Moncrieff (Chatto & Windus, 1949)

Rabelais, Francis, *Gargantua*, trans. Sir Thomas Urquart and P. Le Motteux (Oxford University Press, 1934)

Scotland Today (Scottish Office and Central Office of Information, 1974)

Smith, Adam, *An Inquiry into the Nature and Causes of the Wealth of Nations* (Adam Black & William Tait, 1828)

Smith, Sydney Goodsir, *Collected Poems, 1941–1975* (Calder, 1975)

Stevenson, Robert Louis, *Weir of Hermiston* (Dent, 1925)

Sussex, Elizabeth, *The Rise and Fall of British Documentary* (University of California Press, 1975)

Timpson, George F. (ed), *Sir James A. H. Murray* (John Bellows, 1957)

Weis, Charles McC., and Pottle, Frederick A. (eds), *Boswell in Extremes, 1776–1778* (Heinemann, 1971)

Woodruff, Philip, *The Founders*, The Men who Ruled India, vol 1 (Jonathan Cape, 1953)

Young, Andrew McLaren, *Glasgow University's Pictures* (P. & D. Colnaghi & University of Glasgow Press, 1973)